WIDER HORIZONS OF
AMERICAN HISTORY

WIDER HORIZONS OF AMERICAN HISTORY

HERBERT E. BOLTON

UNIVERSITY OF NOTRE DAME PRESS

NOTRE DAME

First American Paperback Edition 1967
University of Notre Dame Press

Reprinted by special arrangement with
Appleton-Century-Crofts, Division of Meredith Publishing Company

Manufactured in the United States of America
Library of Congress Catalog Card Number: 67-14884

CONTENTS

EDITOR'S FOREWORD

Professor Bolton's four studies have a special claim to a place in this Series, not only because they represent the ripe fruit of his scholarship, but because of the pioneering character of their approach. They represent an interpretation of American history in a new light, revealing those larger horizons within which the cultural elements of the major national groups that contributed to the making of the history of the Americas find their proper place.

The Editors of *New Spain and the Anglo-American West* say of him and his work:

"Trained by such famous historians as Frederick Jackson Turner and John Bach McMaster, Professor Bolton has broken away almost entirely from the methods of presenting American history which were in vogue during his student days. It is true that his interest in the West has continued, but new ideas, facts and interpretations appear in his studies of New Spain and his broader view of the history of both North and South America. He was one of the first to discard the narrowly national method of historical presentation and to recognize the fundamental unity of New World development. American history with him is not merely the story of the thirteen English colonies and the United States, but a more correctly proportioned narrative of the western hemisphere in all its international aspects. . . ." This larger frame-work for American history, which reaches across and beyond national boundaries, appeared first in his *Colonial History of North America* done in collaboration with Thomas M. Marshall, and has since been expounded year after year at the University of California to an enthusiastic group of nearly one thousand students.

Wider Horizons of American History sets forth the larger aspects of Western Hemisphere history. Each essay was prepared for an important occasion, and represents the author's thinking under stimulating circumstances.

Dr. Bolton's whole career has been devoted to broadening and enriching the concept of American history by ransacking unused archives, following new lines of research, and directing many young scholars in American history into new by-ways, some of which they have transformed into highways.

"The Epic of Greater America," the first of the four essays contained in *Wider Horizons,* was Dr. Bolton's presidential address delivered in December, 1932, at Toronto, Canada, before the American

[viii]

Historical Association, where it made a profound impression. It presents in broad synthesis the panorama of Western Hemisphere history as a whole, cutting across national boundaries and pointing out unities, contrasts, and interrelations between the different portions of the Continent.

"Defensive Spanish Expansion and the Significance of the Borderlands" was delivered before the Boulder Conference on the History of the Trans-Mississippi West in June, 1929. It is at once a sweeping sketch and a penetrating interpretation of the significance of the meeting of two European civilizations in the southern Borderlands, done with breadth of outlook, understanding, and clarity of presentation.

"The Mission as a Frontier Institution in the Spanish-American Colonies" was delivered at the University of California in October, 1917, as the annual Faculty Research Lecture. Like the other essays, it cuts across present-day national boundaries. It interprets the mission as an economic, a social, and a political as well as a religious institution—an affair of the State as well as of the Church. According to a leading critic, the essay has become a classic arousing an entirely new interest in mission history.

"The Black Robes of New Spain," the last essay, extends the horizons of American history in still

[ix]

another direction. The phrase "The Jesuits of North America" has hitherto connoted only the French Jesuits in Canada and the Mississippi Valley. This study reveals in dramatic fashion that there were several times as many Spanish as French Jesuits in North America in colonial days, that their work was both more successful and more permanent, and that they left a larger contribution to colonial literature than their French brethren who labored in North America. Delivered in Washington before the Catholic Historical Association in December, 1934, the essay presents much new and illuminating material on this little-known activity of the Jesuit Fathers.

Heretofore to be had only as periodical articles, these essays nevertheless received much favorable attention and exercised a wide influence both in this country and abroad. Their publication in this volume therefore meets a real demand, and will be a source of gratification to many.

AUTHOR'S PREFACE

THE cultures of Western Europe, whence those of the modern Americas have been derived, are as varied as their backgrounds. Yet of them none can stand alone, for in the vast churning process of the centuries each of them has been affected and shaped by contact with its neighbors. Taken together, they constitute an indivisible web, whose many colors suggest diversity of origin as they constitute the pattern of their collective civilization.

Out of these cultures came the Americas, bearing as they came the impress of their common qualities and their local diversities. In new environments, as they took root, they reproduced old patterns and revealed what appeared, because of new scale, to be new patterns. And in the New World, as in the Old, none of them stood quite alone. Only in connection with the neighbors, and in connection with the common environment, can their structure be studied in its full detail.

There is room, in all of the new countries as in all of the old, for the study of chains of sequences tied down to groups and to regions. But above all this there is need for a study of the whole, greater than the sum of its parts, which is the history of the Americas.

The essays comprising this volume were written in an order essentially the reverse of that in which they are here printed. The synthesis presented in the first paper emerged as a resultant of many special researches. Years ago, when I began my historical studies, undertaken as parts of the history of the United States, I soon found that none of them would stay within national boundaries. Whatever subject I touched, it cut across present-day borders, which, of course, are very recent entities.

Out of this experience it eventually occurred to me that the history of all North America is so intertwined that a synthetic study of it would be illuminating. It was this which led me in collaboration with Dr. Thomas M. Marshall, one of my pupils, to sketch out a larger framework for early North American history. That book was only half finished when I realized that not North America alone, but the whole Western Hemisphere, had common historical threads, a presentation of which in synthesis would throw new light upon the development of any one of its component parts.

The first essay here presented sketches in broad outline some of these larger aspects of New World history. The papers which follow are generalized treatments of special aspects of Western Hemisphere genesis touched upon more briefly in the introductory essay. They are three of the numerous studies out of which the general synthesis emerged, and which, taken together, have revealed to me the value of an all-American background for the study of the separate history of any of the various American nations, and for an understanding of inter-American relations.

HERBERT E. BOLTON

Berkeley, April 2, 1939

THE EPIC OF GREATER AMERICA *

I

THE membership of the American Historical Association used to consist almost exclusively of residents of the United States. At the time when it was formed a more exact name for the organization would have been "The United States Historical Association." In recent years the situation has changed. The interests of the body have greatly expanded, and membership has come to include numerous citizens of other American countries, especially of Canada. This widening of the clientele and of the outlook of the Association, together with the holding of the present annual meeting in a Canadian city, would seem to give special fitness to a presidential address dealing with some of the larger aspects of Western Hemisphere history. I have therefore chosen for my subject this evening, The Epic of Greater America.

There is need of a broader treatment of Ameri-

* Presidential Address delivered at the Forty-seventh Annual Meeting of the American Historical Association, December 27–29, 1932, in Toronto, Canada. Printed in the American Historical Review, April, 1933.

[1]

can history, to supplement the purely nationalistic presentation to which we are accustomed. European history cannot be learned from books dealing alone with England, or France, or Germany, or Italy, or Russia; nor can American history be adequately presented if confined to Brazil, or Chile, or Mexico, or Canada, or the United States. In my own country the study of thirteen English colonies and the United States in isolation has obscured many of the larger factors in their development, and helped to raise up a nation of chauvinists. Similar distortion has resulted from the teaching and writing of national history in other American countries.

It is time for a change. The increasing importance of inter-American relations makes imperative a better understanding by each of the history and the culture of all. A synthetic view is important not alone for its present-day political and commercial implications; it is quite as desirable from the standpoint of correct historiography.[1]

For some three hundred years the whole Western Hemisphere was colonial in status. European peoples occupied the country, transplanted their cultures, and adapted themselves to the American scene. Rival nations devised systems for exploiting natives and natural resources, and competed for profit and possession. Some of the contestants were eliminated, leaving at the end of the eighteenth cen-

[2]

tury Spain, Portugal, England, and Russia as the chief colonial powers in the New World.

By this time most of the European colonies in America had grown up; they now asserted their majority. In the half century between 1776 and 1826, practically all of South America and two-thirds of North America became politically independent of Europe, and a score of nations came into being. Eventually, the entire Western Hemisphere, with minor exceptions, has achieved independent nationality. Since separation from Europe these nations alike have been striving on the one hand for national solidarity, political stability, and economic well being, and on the other hand for a satisfactory adjustment of relations with each other and with the rest of the world.

Our national historians, especially in the United States, are prone to write of these broad phases of American history as though they were applicable to one country alone. It is my purpose, by a few bold strokes, to suggest that they are but phases common to most portions of the entire Western Hemisphere; that each local story will have clearer meaning when studied in the light of the others; and that much of what has been written of each national history is but a thread out of a larger strand.

[3]

II

Columbus drew the curtain of the American stage not for Spaniards alone, but for all the European players. This navigator himself seems to have been international, if we may judge from the number of his birthplaces. His daring voyage set in motion a race for the Orient in which several nations took part. The Cabots for England reached the shores of northeastern America and returned home with boats smelling of fish. Portuguese adventurers, sailing around Africa, reached India and set up an empire there. Spain, finding the American continent in the way, sought a route through or around the unexpected nuisance. When Magellan found a southern strait for Spain, Verrazano and Cartier for France, and Thorne for England, in imitation scurried to find a passage farther north. Spain set the fashion; the others tried to keep the pace.

Discovery was followed by exploitation and colonization. This, likewise, was not a matter of one nation, but of many. Spain and Portugal led the way. They not only explored and exploited, but they colonized extensively and permanently, and their experience was utilized by later comers. In rapid succession Spain occupied the West Indies, Central America, Mexico, and all South America

[4]

except the eastern seaboard. There Brazil is an imposing monument to tiny Portugal. On the mainland Spaniards first settled among the advanced peoples—Mayas, Aztecs, Pueblos, Chibchas, and Incas. These natives were easiest to conquer, were most worth exploiting, and their women made the best cooks. It happened, too, that most areas of advanced native culture were regions rich in mineral deposits.

The dominant position of Spain and Portugal in America at the end of the sixteenth century was truly remarkable. No other European power had established a single permanent settlement. Portugal monopolized the Brazilian seaboard. Spain had colonies all the way from Buenos Aires to the Rio Grande. Two-thirds of the Western Hemisphere was then Hispanic, and so it has remained to this day. Spain's exalted position in the New World at the time is illustrated by the enemies who then rose up against her.

The North European countries and France founded no permanent American colonies in the sixteenth century. But all were interested in expansion in similar ways. All took to the sea. All desired a share in the trade of America and the Far East. All tried to break down the monopoly of Spain and Portugal. All made intrusions into the Caribbean and the South American mainland. Britons braved

winds and ice floes in an effort to find a Northwest
Passage. French sea dogs, Dutch sea dogs, and
English sea dogs alike plundered vessels and sacked
towns all round the Hispanic American periphery.
In defence Spain adopted a commercial fleet system, formed a West Indian armada, and walled her
towns on the Caribbean coasts. One of these staunch
old defences tourists see today at Cartagena. The
fortifications at Havana and St. Augustine had a
similar origin. The French intruded into Brazil,
Carolina, and Florida, but were effectively expelled
from all three. Raleigh attempted to found colonies
in Carolina; his Orinoco project sent him to the
block. Drake became a millionaire by plundering
Spaniards, was crowned Great Hioh by the Indians
near San Francisco Bay, and talked of a New Al-
bion in California, long before there was a New
England on the Atlantic Coast.

Then a new chapter opened. At the dawn of the
seventeenth century North Europe and France began to found permanent colonies in the Caribbean
and on the North American mainland. Being late
comers, they established themselves in the leftover
areas. We Saxon Americans today may regard our
respective countries as Promised Lands, reserved
for God's chosen peoples. But our Saxon ancestors
froze and starved in them primarily because their
Hispanic contemporaries were firmly intrenched

[6]

in the sunnier climes. The late comers made vigorous and long-continued attempts to get a foothold on the long Atlantic seaboard of South America, but found the way blocked by the Portuguese.[2] This is one of the chapters we forget.

The favorite colonies of the late comers at the outset were those planted in the Caribbean and Guiana. French, Dutch, English, and Danes settled side by side in the Lesser Antilles, jostled each other, and warred with Spain. They established tropical plantations, trading stations, and buccaneering bases. Till the end of the century, investors' profits were vastly greater here than on the mainland. In 1676 the immigrant population of little Barbados alone was larger than that of all New England.

But the future for these new comers was in the northern continent, with its wide expanse, and its unappropriated back country. Here North Europe and France might hope to achieve something of the renown and a fraction of the wealth which Hispanic Europe had won in Mexico and South America. So France, Holland, Sweden, and England all planted colonies on the northern main.

The details need not detain us. France occupied Acadia, the St. Lawrence Valley, the Alabama and Mississippi basins, and the Canadian prairies. The Swedes and the Dutch settled on the Delaware and the Hudson. England founded subtropical plantations in the South, diversified colonies on the Dutch and Swedish foundations, a coastwise and industrial society in New England, fishing stations in the northeastern waters, and fur trading posts about the shores of Hudson Bay. New England was redolent of fish and brimstone; New France at first was largely a matter of skins and souls—the skins of beaver and the souls of the heathen.

Thus by the end of the seventeenth century European colonies and trading posts formed a fringe like a figure eight clear around the rim of both Americas, from Hudson Bay to the head of the Gulf of California. Middle America was occupied from ocean to ocean, and long salients had been thrust into the interior of the wider continental areas. England alone had not thirteen but nearly thirty colonies in the islands and on the Atlantic seaboard, strung all the way from Guiana to Hudson Bay. As commonly used, the phrase "Original Thirteen" has been very misleading. It does not mean the original colonies at all, but the original states of the American Union.

In these peripheral regions of the two continents the Europeans settled on the land, adjusted themselves to the American environment, devised systems for utilizing natural resources, and transplanted European cultures. Governments were set up, cities founded, religious institutions perpetuated, schools and colleges begun. The universities of Mexico and Lima date from 1551, the Jesuit College of Quebec, ancestor of Laval University, from 1635, Harvard from 1636, William and Mary from 1695, and Yale from 1701. Till near the end of the eighteenth century not Boston, not New York, not Charleston, not Quebec, but Mexico City was the metropolis of the entire Western Hemisphere.

Likenesses in the colonial systems were more striking than differences. All the nations entertained mercantilistic views of colonies—that is to say, they were for the benefit of their own people. Government at first was of the contemporary European pattern, adapted to the American frontier. Nearly every mother country revived in America some vestige of feudalism—Spain tried the *encomienda,* Portugal the *capitania,* Holland the patroon system, England the proprietary grant, France the seigniory.

In all tropical areas Negro slavery was common. Native policies varied according to the natives. Indian tribes were everywhere used as buffers against European rivals. Intractable Indians were everywhere driven back or killed off. Sedentary tribes were subdued, preserved, and exploited. In

[9]

New Spain they were held in *encomienda;* in South Carolina, Brazil, and Dutch America, and in the island colonies generally they were enslaved; in New France and in mainland English America they were utilized in the fur trade. Europeans who came without their women married native girls. Half breeds were numerous in Hispanic and French America, and squawmen were the rule on all French, Dutch, and English frontiers. In the Chickasaw nation in 1792 a fourth of the one thousand heads of Indian families were white men, mainly English.

In one respect the Indian policies of the Latin countries differed essentially from those of the Saxons. The Latins considered the Indian worth civilizing and his soul worth saving. This was due largely to the influence of the Church. So in Brazil, Spanish America, and New France the missionary played a conspicuous rôle. There Franciscans, Dominicans, Augustinians, Jesuits, and other orders labored on every border, and founded Indian missions and Indian schools. The brilliant Parkman made widely known the heroic work of the Jesuits in New France. Less famous in Saxon circles is the equally heroic and vastly more extensive work of the Jesuits in Spanish and Portuguese America. In colonial Mexico alone there were several times as many Jesuits as in all New France.

III

Beginning on the rim of the continent, these European settlers pushed into the interior, opening new mines, new missions, new plantations, new farms, new trading posts, new administrative jurisdictions. Sometimes the advance into the hinterland was a westward movement, sometimes it was eastward, sometimes southward, sometimes northward. Everywhere contact with frontier environment and native peoples tended to modify the Europeans and their institutions. This was quite as true in the Latin as in the Saxon colonies.

Colonial expansion involved international rivalry. This, too, embraced the entire hemisphere. In Saxon America the story of the "struggle for the continent" has usually been told as though it all happened north of the Gulf of Mexico. But this is just another provincialism of ours. The southern continent was the scene of international conflicts quite as colorful and fully as significant as those in the north.

Minor rivalries occurred in Guiana, where France, Holland, and England exploited the region side by side. England for a century tried without success to break into the Spanish Main, and called into being the viceroyalty of New Granada. Into Portuguese America the French and Dutch intruded with great vigor and dogged tenacity.

But the major contest for territory in the austral continent was between Brazil and her Spanish neighbors to the west and south. Here an empire equal in area to the Mississippi Valley was at stake. By papal grant and royal treaty Portugal was restricted to a narrow strip on the Atlantic shore. So said the documents. But this delimitation made little difference in fact. Snapping their fingers at decrees and treaties, hardy Brazilians pushed their frontiers rapidly west, founded Portuguese settlements in the interior, and plundered Spanish outposts on the Paraguay border. The Brazilian drive toward the Andes strongly resembles the westward movement in the United States and Canada.

Spain contested these inroads. In resisting them the Jesuits played a dramatic part. Their Paraguay missions became a buffer province to restrain the aggressive Portuguese. From middle Paraguay they extended their reductions above the great falls of the Iguazú. There for twenty years they prospered, and then the Portuguese hammer fell upon them. Within three years thousands of mission Indians were carried off as slaves to Brazil. With the remainder—twelve thousand neophytes—Father

Montoya and his associates fled helter-skelter in river craft five hundred miles down the stream, skirting through tropical forests the ninety miles of falls and rapids that broke navigation. This stirring episode antedated by more than a hundred and twenty years the Acadian expulsion which it somewhat resembled, and it determined the fate of a territory vastly greater in size. Striking new root in the south, the Jesuits defended that border for another century, sometimes by open warfare. The left bank of the lower Plata was another scene of long continued give and take. Brazil edged south at her neighbor's expense, but Spain managed to hold the region that became the Republic of Uruguay. The middle eighteenth century saw the border contest come to a head. With English backing, Portugal had the advantage. In 1750 by treaty Brazil was given a boundary much like that of today. Thus the Line of Demarcation, fixed in the time of Columbus and Cabral, was sadly bent, and Brazil came to occupy nearly half of South America.

There was another chapter in this story. To restrain the Portuguese from further encroachments and to keep out the threatening English, who had now occupied the Falkland Islands, Spain established the viceroyalty of La Plata, with its capital at Buenos Aires. This was one of the signifi-

[13]

cant American events of 1776. It did much to de-
termine the destiny of the southern continent.

The scene now shifts to the top of the map. Here
again the story has been distorted through a provincial view of history. The contest for North
America is usually represented as falling between
1689 and 1763, confined chiefly to the valleys of
the Ohio and the St. Lawrence, and ending on
the Plains of Abraham. But this is far too restricted
a view. The story neither opened on the Ohio nor
closed at Quebec.

In eastern North America territorial rivalry began with the first intrusions of other Europeans
into Spanish possessions in the Caribbean. In the
sixteenth century the intruders merely barked at
the Spaniards' heels. In the seventeenth century,
long before 1689, important transfers of territory
were effected both in the islands and on the mainland. By settlement of unoccupied islands, England,
France, and Holland absorbed many regions stubbornly claimed but neglected by Spain. England
conquered Jamaica, and the French took western
Haiti. On the mainland, both Virginia and South
Carolina were settled by England in the face of
Spanish resistance; Swedes on the Delaware and
Dutch on the Hudson soon found themselves in
the maw of the English Lion. For decades the

[14]

buccaneers ravaged Spain's Caribbean shores. Jamaica was the focus; Seitz has epitomized the story in four lines:

Ho! Henry Morgan sails today
To harry the Spanish Main
With a pretty bill for the Dons to pay
Ere he comes back again.

For this harrying Morgan, like Drake, was knighted.

Then followed the more militant rivalry which Parkman has so brilliantly depicted as the *Half Century of Conflict*. It was a death grip of England not with France alone but with both France and Spain for eastern North America. On the northern mainland fur trade and Indian alliances played a significant rôle. In the Caribbean and Georgia the Anglo-Spanish contest still raged. Not only Louisbourg and Quebec, but also Cartagena, Puerto Bello, Havana, and St. Augustine, were targets for English cannon.

The long struggle was marked by five European wars. In each of them nearly all international frontiers were war-zones—the Caribbean, the Spanish Main, the Florida-Carolina border, Acadia, Hudson Bay. In the contest Carolinians duplicated on a smaller scale in Georgia and Florida the savage Portuguese raids on the Spanish mis-

[15]

sions of Paraguay. In one campaign an ex-governor of South Carolina destroyed thirteen Spanish missions, burned Fathers Parga and Miranda at the stake, and carried off more than a thousand mission Indians. Bit by bit England shaved off two borderlands. France yielded her claims to Hudson Bay, Newfoundland, and Acadia; Oglethorpe's intruding colony broke Spain's hold on Georgia. But "Old Grog" Vernon's disaster in the War of Jenkin's Ear checked English designs on the Spanish Main. There Spain remained intact, for yellow fever was a faithful ally of the Dons. Incidentally, through Washington's brother, who served in the Cartagena campaign, this war gave the United States a name for its national shrine, Mt. Vernon.

The final clash with France in this chapter of history came when English settlers threatened the French hold on the Ohio Valley. The classic story needs no repetition here. Leaden plates and a line of posts signalized French determination to hold on. France was encouraged by four years of success; the tide turned when Pitt took the helm for England. With Wolfe's victory on the Plains of Abraham, French rule in mainland North America ended.

But the close of French rule did not remove the Gallic people. Here historians often forget. The French settlers remained, continued to be path-

finders in the West, and their prolific descendants
today constitute a third of Canada's population.
Yankee institutions have edged across the line into
British North America. As an offset, French Canadians have pushed south and contributed greatly
to the economic life of New England.

The end was not yet. The contest for the continent did not close with the Portuguese drive for
the Andes, with the absorption of Spain's Caribbean islands, nor with England's victory at Quebec.
Western North America was similarly involved.
International rivalry was quite as much a feature
of western as of eastern America, even in colonial
days, and its story cannot properly be separated
from the other. The stage for the contest for the
continent was as wide as the hemisphere and its
adjacent seas. It was international rivalry that
brought into existence as organized communities
nearly all the Spanish borderland areas of the
Southwest and the Pacific Coast. These stirring
episodes, if treated at all, have been considered
only as local history, but they are a part of the
general theme. They are no more local history than
is the struggle for the St. Lawrence or the Mississippi Valley.

On her northern borderland Spain's expansion
was largely defensive. The French intruded into

Carolina and Georgia, Menéndez expelled them, and founded Florida. Into Texas Spain was forced by a later French intrusion. La Salle founded his short-lived colony on the Gulf as a base for seizing the mines of Mexico, not primarily, as Parkman says, to hold back the English. Spain, aroused to action, planted temporary settlements in the Piney Woods of eastern Texas. In the course of the contest the Marqués de Aguayo marched a thousand miles, at the head of cavalry raised at his own expense, restored Spain's posts beyond the Trinity, and returned to the Rio Grande on foot, through loss of nearly five thousand horses in a blizzard. Aguayo saved Texas for Spain and made Napoleon's pretension and Jefferson's claim to the province as a part of Louisiana an historical joke. During the same international episode in which Aguayo recovered Texas for Spain, the French advance up the Platte River was met by a Spanish gesture from Santa Fe toward occupying the region which is now eastern Colorado.

Louisiana tells a similar story. The Seven Years' War gave North America a new map west of the Mississippi as well as east of it. At the end of the struggle Spain found herself in possession of half of the former patrimony of France, and frowning at England across the Father of Waters. Acquired by Carlos III in the stress of conflict, Louisiana was occupied and developed by Spain primarily as a buffer province to hold back first the English and then the Anglo-Americans.

Upper California was likewise a child of international rivalry. Jesuit missionaries had carried the Spanish frontier into Arizona and Lower California. There it stood. Then the Russian Bear threatened. Bering explored the North Pacific and Russians planted posts in Alaska. So Spain moved up the map once more. Portolá and Serra planted garrisons and missions at San Diego and Monterey. A few days before the Declaration of Independence was proclaimed in Philadelphia, San Francisco was founded on the Pacific Coast. It was planted as an outpost to hold the northwestern border of Spain's vast empire, a realm which extended from the Strait of Magellan to the Golden Gate. Though less a matter of bullets, the founding of San Francisco was as much a part of world history as was Wolfe's victory at Quebec. It was another of the significant events of 1776.

IV

Then came the American Revolution. This too was by no means a local matter. It lasted half a century—from 1776 to 1826—and it witnessed the political separation of most of America from Europe. The event was perhaps inevitable. Spain, Portugal, and England had founded vigorous colonies. They grew up and asserted their majority. The revolutions were the surest signs that the mother countries had succeeded. Thirteen of the English colonies led the way; Spanish and Portuguese America followed. Throwing off their status as wards, English, Spanish, and Portuguese colonists set themselves up as American nations. Viewed thus broadly the American Revolution takes on larger significance.

Of the revolt of the Thirteen English colonies little need be said before this audience. The causes were inherent in the situation. Beginning as a struggle for redress of grievances, it quickly became a war for independence. Soon the contest became international, a fact which determined the outcome. France, Spain, and Holland joined the colonial cause against England. Spain drove the British soldiery from the lower Mississippi and recovered the Floridas. In the final victory the French navy played a decisive part. The treaty of peace was a shock to European monarchs. It recognized not only a Western Hemisphere nation, but a nation with a democratic form of government. Through hostility to England the rest of Europe had contributed toward the ultimate loss of all colonial

America and toward the undermining of the monarchical system.

The independence of the United States was not fully assured by the surrender at Yorktown. For the next third of a century European interests in the Mississippi Valley were a menace to the continued independence and growth of the new republic. The shadow of Europe lay deep over the West. The infant nation was not born a giant, and many persons of prominence thought it would fail. European powers looked on with interest. If the young upstart ceased to exist, they would be on hand to share the estate; if it survived, they would check its growth and dominate its fortunes. This danger was averted only by the jealousy and the long conflict among the Europeans themselves, and by the vigor of American growth. Spain threatened the Southwest. England occupied an analogous position north of the Ohio. France was more dangerous than either. She hoped to dominate the Ohio Valley, or even to separate it from the United States. In this she failed, but by browbeating Spain, Napoleon regained Louisiana. Then, suddenly, his colonial plans having changed, he sold it to the United States for a song. By 1822 the shadow of Europe in the West was dispelled and independence confirmed.

The revolt of thirteen of the thirty British colonies laid the foundations not of one but of two English speaking nations in North America. One was the United States; the other was the Dominion of Canada. Before 1776 Canada was mainly French in race stock. The settlers who now arrived made up the first large English speaking element in the country. In the revolt of the colonies the people were far from unanimous. Only thirteen of the provinces joined, though appeals were made to all. The Maritime Provinces, Quebec, the two Floridas, and the island colonies, all stood by the mother country. Even in the thirteen a third of the people were opposed to the revolution.

Under harsh treatment by the separatists, thousands of these Loyalists emigrated during and after the war. Going to Halifax became a well recognized pursuit. Some settled in the old Maritime Provinces, and others in newly formed New Brunswick. Still others flocked to Upper Canada—the Ontario of today. So British Canada was largely Yankee in origin. These United Empire Loyalists, founders of this city,[3] and a multitude of others, were Canada's Pilgrim Fathers. It was they who did the most to shape the history of the vast domain north of the United States. The small seed of empire which they planted beside the French colony has grown to be the great Dominion of Canada.

[22]

Two American nations had been founded. But the revolution had only started. At the end of the eighteenth century only a small patch on the American map had won its independence from Europe. Portugal still ruled Brazil, and Spain's power was intact all the way from Patagonia to the borders of Oregon. But the revolution went on.

A third of a century behind the English colonies those of Spain and Portugal arose in revolt. In the two cases there were similarities and contrasts. The causes were in many respects alike. In both movements independence was achieved through outside aid. The area involved in Hispanic was ten times that in English America, and the population several times larger. In Hispanic America there were vastly greater obstacles to united action than in English America. Mountains and distance gave more effective isolation. As a consequence there were separate revolutionary movements in the different areas, and several nations resulted.

External influences played a prominent part in bringing the revolution about. England and France, trade rivals of Spain, plotted the liberation of her colonies. Subversive French philosophy penetrated Spanish America in spite of all efforts to keep it out. Young Creoles were educated in Europe. English and American contact through smuggling spread liberal ideas. The revolt of the English colo-

[23]

nies, the French Revolution, and the independence of Santo Domingo furnished examples. Napoleon started the ball a-rolling by seating his brother Joseph on the throne of Spain. Spanish American resistance to the French usurper soon changed into a war for separation from the mother country.

Independence came to Brazil without bloodshed. Here as in Spanish America, Napoleon set things in motion. When he threatened to depose the Braganzas in Portugal, John, Prince Regent, fled with his court to Brazil. By his liberal policy he stirred new life in the quiescent colony. Brazil became a kingdom, John returned to Portugal and left his son Pedro as regent. Brazil and Portugal now grew apart. Ordered home, Pedro refused to go, raised the *Grito de Ypiranga,* declared for independence, and became emperor (1822).

The wars of independence in Spanish South America were an imposing military drama. Miranda the Precursor led the way in Venezuela. Bolívar the Liberator assumed his mantle. For fifteen years this brilliant figure moved back and forth across the continent, setting up republics, defeated here, winning victories there. Then for a time the revolution was nearly stamped out. But Bolívar had a way of coming back. Aided by British volunteers—veterans released after Napoleon's fall—he crossed the Andes where they are thirteen thousand feet high, routed the royalists, and completed the revolution in Colombia. This Washington of South America well merited his title of *El Libertador*. In the North the dominating figure of Bolívar gave unity to the war. In the South there was less cohesion, but the cause prevailed. By 1816 the Argentine was practically free. Dr. Francia expelled the royalists and set up a republic in Paraguay. In the Banda Oriental Artigas, the picturesque Gaucho chieftain, laid the foundations of Uruguayan nationality. The rebel forces of the North and the South now closed in on Peru, the last royalist stronghold. San Martín, greatest soldier of the South, forged a new army at Mendoza, made a stupendous march over the Andes by awe-inspiring Uspallata Pass, and completed the revolution in Chile. Then, with fresh forces, carried north in a fleet commanded by a British admiral, he defeated the royalists at Lima, and turned his army over to the Liberator. Bolívar ascended the Andes, created the Republic of Bolivia, and ended the war in Spanish South America. Bolivia commemorates his name.

Simultaneously with these epic events North America ended the rule of Spain. Hidalgo rang the Liberty Bell and sounded the *Grito de Dolores*. Mexican schoolboys still bless him because he raised the cry precisely at midnight, for in order to be sure to celebrate the right day, both the fifteenth and the sixteenth of September are national holidays. The Philadelphia bell-ringer was not so considerate. Hidalgo raised an armed mob, defeated the royalists, and seized government stores. Routed at Guadalajara, he fled north, was captured, and executed at Chihuahua. Rayón rose and fell. Then emerged Morelos, mule-driver priest, the chief military figure of the war in Mexico. His astounding victories were followed by a declaration of independence.

The revolt had spread like a flash to the northern provinces of New Spain, where it was given special character by the proximity of the United States. It must be remembered that at this time the Floridas, Texas, all the Southwest, and California were still wards of Spain. Occurrences there which in the nationalistic mold have been regarded as local events, in this larger perspective are seen to be important phases of the history of the New World.

The people of the United States favored the Mexican revolution. They had recently fought one themselves, and were flattered by the imitation. They were interested in the spread of democracy, in Mexican commerce, and in Mexican land. Sam Houston of Tennessee, long before he became famous in Texas, offered to join the revolutionary cause there in return for real estate. There were boundary disputes between the United States and Spain, and now was a good time to settle them. So Mexico found many a helping hand. President Madison encouraged a revolution in West Florida, but when a republic was erected there he seized the district to keep order and to forestall England, for the War of 1812 was now in progress. In East Florida Madison fostered another short-lived revolt, with a similar purpose in view. Carolinians and Georgians ravaged the province but were expelled. Texas was "liberated" by a volunteer army raised in the United States, but was reconquered by Spain.

Meanwhile in Mexico the revolutionary congress fled from place to place, much as the Continental Congress had done before it. Heroic Morelos was captured and executed. But the revolt, now stamped out in the center, was kept alive on the frontiers. Here Western Hemisphere history was being made. Mina revived the spark by a raid from Texas. Andrew Jackson embarrassed Spain by invading East Florida, for Bahama Britons threatened. Uncle Sam took advantage of Spain's predicament to acquire title to both Floridas, which he already held by military force,[4] and to negotiate the boundary line of 1819. General Long led new expeditions from the United States into Texas, and set up a temporary republic. Galveston Island continued to be a base for proclamations and revolutionary raids. Bouchard, by an expedition that sailed all the way from Argentina, tried in vain to arouse contented California. On the far southern fringe of Mexico Guerrero kept up a guerrilla warfare. All these border disturbances, which are usually treated as local events, were parts of the greater American Revolution.

Iturbide now brought the struggle to a climax. Sent by royalists to crush Guerrero, he joined hands with the rebel instead, and ended the rule of Spain. Then, making himself emperor, he carried the war of liberation into Central America. He in turn was soon overthrown, and the republic of Mexico was established, though shorn of the Floridas, eastern Texas, and Central America. The American Revolution had been fought and won. It did not end at Yorktown.

It was these events that called forth the Monroe Doctrine and that make it intelligible. European monarchs looked askance at the large crop of American republics. After the overthrow of Napoleon, that mutual insurance society at one stage called the Holy Alliance was formed to restore legitimate sovereigns. It essayed this task in Spain and in Italy, and then discussed the reconquest of Spanish America. Just then Russia took an aggressive position regarding the Pacific Northwest. The czar

declared the North Pacific a closed sea. In reply
Monroe issued his famous dictum, denouncing further colonization of America by Europe and all
plans to restore monarchy here. Russia now withdrew her claims below 54° 40′—hence the phrase
later used as a campaign slogan—and the allies
gave up their plans to restore Spanish rule in America. England's precise part in this episode is still
a subject of debate.

In most of the new Hispanic states independence was followed by disorder—like the "Critical
Period" in the history of the United States. The
turbulence was due to political inexperience, class
antipathies, geographical barriers, and sectional or
personal ambitions. But the struggle was not mean-
ingless chaos. In the long period of strife, cleavage
in politics usually centered on fundamental issues:
centralism versus federalism; civilian rule versus
militarism; privilege versus opportunity.

Disorder led to one man power. Mysterious
Francia in Paraguay, bloody Rosas in Argentina,
and venal Santa Anna in Mexico are examples of
caudillos or military chiefs who thus became dicta-
tors. The struggle for nationality in Spanish America during the first half century after independence
is typified by the fortunes of Mexico. There disorder and inexperience led not only to dictatorship

but also to foreign invasion and loss of territory. Mexico's career was given special character, and made more difficult, by proximity to the "Colossus of the North."

V

Saxon America again occupied the center of the Western Hemisphere stage. All the Old World and the New anxiously watched the drama. The theme of the play was the completion of the map. By the time the Hispanic states were established their territorial limits were fairly well fixed except on the north. The Spanish republics fitted into the *audiencia* districts of the old viceroyalties, whose outlines were already determined. Since independence there have been many boundary disputes in Hispanic America, Brazil has taken good-sized bites out of her neighbors' domain, but there have been few major transfers of territory.

Quite different was the case of Saxon America. When independence came to the United States and the Loyalists founded British Canada, most of North America above Mexico was still in the raw. Spain's holdings north of the Rio Grande were mainly defensive and missionary outposts. Beyond these, the major portion of the continent was Indian country, still in the fur trade stage. It lay in the pathway of several expanding peoples. It was a frontier of four empires, each of which contributed its pioneers. It was their land of opportunity, and it was anybody's prize. The ultimate domains of the three principal North American nations were still to be hammered out. The shaping of them was a primary interest of the Hemisphere for the next half century. Western North America was still largely a matter of frontiersmen and international politics. The spoils to be divided were the Spanish borderlands and the open spaces of the great West and Northwest. It was an affair of all North America, not of any single nation. The outcome no one could predict, patriotic historians to the contrary notwithstanding.

In this elemental process of shaping national zones the two English speaking peoples moved westward side by side. In each there was a succession of frontier types. In both cases the vanguard were the fur men. The United States frontier nosed its way like a wedge between British America on the right flank and Spanish America on the left. Besides being the crux of international relations, both border zones were areas of cultural influence, quite as significant as that of the isolated frontier.

Into the Pacific Northwest, British and American fur men raced across the continent. These "splendid wayfarers" profited by the commerce in

[31]

skins, marked out spheres of influence for their respective nations, prepared the way for fixing boundaries, and were harbingers of permanent civilization. The British traders moved west from two eastern bases, and represented principally two great organizations. The Hudson's Bay Company at first held close to eastern shores. In the mid-eighteenth century it was forced inland by French rivalry in the back country and by criticism at home.[5] Then it found a new rival in the St. Lawrence Valley. Scotch settlers entered the fur trade at Montreal, formed the Northwest Company, and pushed boldly west. Mackenzie, McGillivray, McDougal, and all the rest—they have been called the "Clan of the Macks." South of the Great Lakes they competed with American traders and beyond the Mississippi they invaded the territory of Spain. In the Minnesota country and on the Missouri the Americans found them intrenched in the Louisiana Purchase. In the Canadian prairies the Nor'westers engaged in a life and death struggle with the Hudson's Bay Company. Rival posts were planted on every important stream. Price wars and bloodshed ensued, and tribal relations were sadly upset. But important explorations resulted; the Rocky Mountains were soon reached, and Mackenzie descended his fluvial namesake to the Arctic Ocean.

The next step in the march was across the north-

ern Rockies. Mackenzie again led the way and rivals followed. Spaniards from St. Louis ascended
the Missouri, and Lewis and Clark crossed the
mountains to the Lower Columbia. For the Nor'-
westers Fraser established posts in Fraser River
Valley and David Thompson got a toe-hold on the
upper Columbia in regions which are now British
Columbia, Idaho, and Montana. Fraser's New Cal-
edonia posts were the first permanent English speaking settlements on the Pacific Coast of America.
Close behind the Nor'westers went Astor's men,
and when Thompson descended the Columbia to
its mouth he found Astoria established there. For
the moment he was forestalled.

Then the American fur men had a setback. To
them the War of 1812 was disastrous all along the
border from Detroit to Astoria. Indians around the
Lakes generally joined the British, and American
traders fell back. Manuel Lisa and his associates retreated down the Missouri. Astoria was sold to the
Nor'westers to prevent its capture by a British war
vessel.

Canadian fur men were now confident. The Oregon country was already in their hands. Why not
restore the good old boundary of the Quebec Act,
and extend it west? Urged by the traders, the British
peace commissioners at Ghent proposed just this,
demanding the cession of most of the country north

[33]

of the Ohio, Missouri, and Platte rivers. It would have been a pretty slice of territory. But quite the contrary happened, and the Canadians in turn got a setback. By the treaty British fur men were excluded from the United States, American traders replaced them around the Lakes, and the boundary was run along the forty-ninth parallel to the Rockies. Another great chapter in the story of the map was finished. As the Americans saw it, the shadow of Britain in the Upper Mississippi Valley had been removed. Canadians express it differently.

West of the Rockies the Canadians were still far ahead. Spain traded her rights to Oregon for those to Texas and withdrew south to 42°. Then Mexico took Spain's place. England and the United States arranged for joint occupation of the Oregon country —a nine hundred mile stretch from California to 54° 40'. In that vast region the legal rights of the two nations were now equal. But *de facto* the advantage was clearly with the British, for the Astorians had sold out, and left the British in control. Nor'westers now consolidated with the Hudson's Bay Company, a western capital was placed at Fort Vancouver,[6] and Dr. McLoughlin took charge. For nearly two decades now this white-haired factor controlled most of the fur business of the Pacific Northwest, all the way from San Francisco to Alaska and eastward to the Rockies. His Russian counterpart at

Sitka was Baránof. These two fur barons were dic-
tators of all Northwest America.

The American fur men had better luck in Mexico. Forestalled by the British traders in the Oregon
country, they pushed southwest and west across the
Great Valley and into the Rockies. Everywhere
west of Louisiana and south of 42° they were intruders on Mexican soil. Most of our American explorer heroes of the Far West, from Smith to Frémont, were in reality belated explorers of a foreign
country. For a quarter century after 1820 these trespassers roamed the western wilds, profiting by the
fur trade, and "discovering" the mountain passes—
which Spaniards had discovered long before. Into
the Great Basin they entered simultaneously by way
of the Platte River and the Rio Grande.

These mountain men were exemplars of manifest
destiny. They wandered through Mexican lands,
sometimes with but more generally without permission, unconscious of their character as unwelcome
intruders, or arrogantly resentful of dark-skinned
people who spoke a foreign tongue and disputed the
"inalienable right" of Americans to do as they
pleased. Most of the fur gatherers were restless
adventure lovers—rolling stones who gathered no
moss—nor can we say that they got a very fine polish
in the process of rolling. But they were endowed
with that physical energy, that fondness for a life of

half savagery, and that detachment from locality which fitted them for the great task which Titanic Nature had set for someone.

Below the impresario Americans, who as partners managed large affairs, and beside the rank and file of reckless Americans who went as hired men or free trappers, there were the more numerous French *engagés*. These hardy souls, half European, half Indian, still formed the backbone of the western fur trade both in Canada and the United States. One such has given his name to Provo, another to Laramie, another to Pierre's Hole. Western Canada is similarly peppered with place-names commemorating the deeds of the French. These half-breeds did the humbler tasks of rowing, packing, skin curing, and camp duty. They served as guides into the wilderness, for their ancestors for generations had led the van, whether under French, English, Spanish, or American rule. Just as the American cowboy learned his trade from the Spanish *vaquero,* so the American fur trader borrowed his methods and his lingo from the French *métis*. *Bourgeois,* the word for manager, in the mouth of the mountain men became *bushwa,* for boss.

These American fur men were by no means monarchs of all they surveyed. In the southern Rockies and in the Great Basin they found Mexican traders

everywhere ahead of them. They tried to push into
jointly owned Oregon, but found their way blocked
by the Hudson's Bay Company, safely intrenched
in Snake River Valley. Climbing the Sierras, they
descended the western slopes into California. There,
in the Sacramento Valley, they found the streams
trapped by Russians from Fort Ross and by Mc-
Loughlin's brigades from Fort Vancouver. A Hudson's Bay settlement encountered by the Americans
in the valley, and for obvious reasons called by them
French Camp, is still in existence near Stockton and
still bears the same name.

The Americans had been beaten, not only to the
Pacific Northwest, but to northern California as
well. Both they and the men of H.B.C. were unwelcome trespassers on the soil of Mexico. The international contest was not yet over. The map was not
yet made. The ultimate fate of the Far West was
still in doubt. Spain was out, Russia had backed up
to 54° 40′, but England, the United States, and Mexico still had their stake. When the republic of Texas
was created, it, too, developed ambitions for a frontage on the Pacific.

The uncertainty was removed by the settler. Fur
men and Santa Fe trader were followed into the
alluring regions by land hungry Americans. All that
had gone before, all the colonial and international

drama of the centuries, was the background into which fitted the relentless westward movement of the farmer frontier.

By 1820 the United States had achieved stability and confirmed its independence from Europe. The next two decades witnessed the rise of the great Middle West and the formation of a western democracy. It was a militant democracy, fully imbued with belief in manifest destiny. American institutions must embrace and regenerate the entire Western Hemisphere. A concrete application was to be found in the rich lands of Mexico and the disputed Oregon country, just beyond. So the shadow of Europe in the West now gave way to the shadow of the United States in the West—a specter which all America and several European nations viewed with anxiety, for nearly half of the northern continent was still at stake. Impelled by this expansion urge, Anglo-Americans drove a wide salient between Canada and Mexico, checking the expansion of one, and absorbing half the territory of the other. This madness for conquest has been called by our southern neighbors "the other side of the Monroe Doctrine."

Mexico, in spite of her turmoil, likewise felt the impulse of expansion. Settlers poured into her northern provinces at a rate unprecedented under Spain. The vast "Spanish Grants," as they are erroneously called, in Texas, New Mexico, Colorado, and California, were nearly all made during the Mexican régime. Part of the new settlers were Mexicans; part were foreigners. Spain had invited Anglo-Americans into Florida and Louisiana. Mexico now made the same political mistake in Texas, New Mexico, and California.

Many factors aroused American interest in the Far West. Boston coast traders, overland fur men, Northwestern missionaries, and official explorers had spied out the land. Interest was stimulated by sectional rivalry, and by fear of England, France, or Russia. Pathfinders beckoned; government tried to follow. By diplomacy, through purchase from Mexico and through compromise with England, it essayed to acquire all the vast region between Louisiana and the Pacific. Mexico did not wish to sell, and England was "stubborn"—so our schoolbooks say. Canning put his heavy foot down on the Columbia, and there he stood; so Uncle Sam resorted to watchful waiting. We thank President Wilson for the phrase, for it precisely fits the case. Wilkes, Ap Jones, Larkin, and Frémont all typify the government's hope that something would "turn up" and give the coveted area to Uncle Sam.

While government watched, settlers moved in. Invited, Americans colonized Texas, arose in revolt, and sought annexation, alternating this ambition with dreams of possessing "the fine harbor of Monterey." Covered wagons creaked their way from the Middle West to Oregon; then England and the United States divided the disputed area. Uninvited, and long before the Gold Rush, other covered wagons invaded California, still a part of Mexico; their occupants obtained generous land grants, and then, imitating the Texans, they set up the Bear Flag Republic. When something thus turned up, Frémont was on hand. Uninvited, Mormons poured into Utah, also Mexican territory. Uncle Sam's soldiers and diplomats now supplemented the work of the settlers. Texas was annexed; Mexico went to war, and was forced to yield half of her domain. The purchase of the Gadsden strip and of Alaska completed the story of Saxon territorial growth on the western mainland. The contest for the continent was practically over.

This partition of the western seaboard of North America was highly significant. It cut off from Spanish America the remaining borderland areas which had been only partly Hispanized and placed the boundary near the frontier of effective Spanish colonization. It gave both Canada and the United States a frontage on the Pacific. It enabled them both to assimilate added millions of Europeans. Built on the national domain, in both countries the West became a powerful nationalizing force. The process of growth kept both nations young with continued frontier experience; it prolonged opportunity for social experimentation, and perpetuated early American and Canadian characteristics.

VI

On this long colonial and international background the subsequent development of the Western Hemisphere was founded. The nations had come into being. The outline of the map had been essentially completed. The territorial bases for the national system had been laid. The next phase was the filling in of the spaces with people, national unification, and economic growth. Like all the earlier phases, this, too, was not confined to one American nation, but was hemisphere wide.

In this whole process of national growth and unification in the nineteenth century the outstanding factors were boundless natural resources, foreign immigration, foreign capital, and expanding markets. Without these, none of the American nations would have come far on the road which they have traveled. No time is left me for detail, and I can only indicate the broad lines. But if you are like my students, I am sure you will gladly forgive me for what I leave out.

The United States first got under way. Here ter-

ritorial expansion was attended by growing pains.
Tariffs, the slavery question, the acquisition of
Texas, Oregon, and California aroused sectional
jealousies. For thirty years peace between the sec-
tions was maintained by compromise. War followed, but the Union was preserved. It was then
multiplied in strength by the peopling of the Far
West. Wide flung and sprawling, it was welded by
the building of transcontinental railroads, the economic reconstruction of the South, and the reor-
ganization of industry on a national scale. In all
this, European immigration and European capital
played a decisive part. By the end of the nineteenth
century both political and economic nationality had
been achieved.

While the United States were gaining solidarity
and power, the British provinces to the north were
being similarly welded into a great dominion. The
War of 1812 stimulated their sense of nationality,
and British immigration lessened American influence. By 1850 the provinces had already won re-
sponsible government, but they were still detached
entities. Like the United States, the Dominion was
fashioned out of scraps of territory variously acquired.

Now the tide of federation set strongly in. Union
was prompted by community of interests. Obstacles
were met in local hostilities and racial suspicion.

Federation found able champions and determined opponents. There were Hamiltons and Calhouns. In the Quebec Conference—as significant in Canadian history as the Constitutional Convention in the United States—the Dominion of Canada was born. One by one the older provinces joined. *A mari usque ad mare* became the slogan. Hudson's Bay Company relinquished its vast jurisdiction in the West, Manitoba and British Columbia entered the union, and the Dominion did indeed extend from sea to sea.

The loosely knit federation, like its neighbor a little earlier, was now welded by transcontinental railroads and the development of the West. The American movement to the frontier was duplicated in Canada. European capital furnished the means. European immigrants thronged, Americans flocked across the border, new prairie provinces were formed, Winnipeg and Vancouver became boom towns. New railroads built up still more northerly cities, and mining rushes developed the yet more remote Northwest. Like California, Oregon and Washington, British Columbia looks out across the Pacific.

The World War stimulated Canadian loyalism on the one hand, and English conciliation on the other. Canada now has full membership in the British Commonwealth of Nations. A fine sentiment binds her to the empire, but she is in all essentials an independent nation. From pole to pole American independence from Europe has been achieved.

Hispanic America has a similar tale of national growth to tell. Some of our southern neighbors have been moving rapidly along the same road as that traveled by the Anglo-American nations. The last half century has been remarkable especially for the emergence of the ABC powers—Argentina, Brazil, and Chile.

The essential factors in the recent development of these countries are much the same as those which have operated in Canada and the United States. Foreign capital and foreign immigration have been decisive. Italians, Spaniards, and Germans have come to the ABC countries by millions to make their homes. Railroads, plantations, stock ranches, nitrate works, mines, and oil wells have been developed by English and German funds. In business matters Uncle Sam has by no means had a monopoly there. Will Rogers, whom all will accept as an authority, wrote from Buenos Aires a few years ago, "Englishmen have got this country sewed up tighter than Borah has Idaho." Other indexes of material progress in that far Southland are the great modern cities, such as Santiago, Rio de Janeiro, and São Paulo. Cultural progress has followed material prosperity. Buenos Aires, with its nearly three million inhabitants, is the third city in the Western Hemisphere, and one of the great ones of the world. Brazil, with a population of over forty millions, is the second power in America, a title which Argentina probably would contest. When a Brazilian boasted of his country's forty-three millions, an Argentinian retorted, "You must have counted all those who live in the trees."

"The first shall be last!" In the tropics and around the shores of the Caribbean there has been less material progress than in the temperate regions. The areas which were most developed in early colonial days are now most retarded.[7] Nevertheless, backwardness is only relative, and some of these tropical regions, with their fruit, oil, and other resources, have recently attracted capital and been developed at a tremendous rate. There a score of cities are fast forging into notice as centers of a surprisingly vigorous economic and cultural life.

Mexico, our nearest Hispanic neighbor, has continued to have its ups and downs. The fall of Maximilian was followed by the rule of one of the remarkable men of all time. Porfirio Díaz, half-breed Zapotec Indian, and soldier hero, became president on the platform of no reëlection—and then held office for seven terms in succession. He was a benevolent despot. He gave Mexico what it then most lacked—good order and material progress. Foreign capital poured in, railroads were built, mines and oil wells opened. What had happened in the United States, Canada, and Brazil, was duplicated there. Díaz became a much eulogized world figure. Outsiders saw Mexico in a Golden Age.

But prosperity was one-sided. Vast estates were still intact while millions of people needed land. Foreigners and the old aristocracy flourished while peons were still bound to the soil. The kettle of unrest boiled, and the lid blew off. Madero gave the new *Grito,* Díaz fled the country never to return, Madero fell, Huerta was eliminated, Carranza put in power, and the new constitution installed. Socialistic and nationalistic in its aims, fifteen years have been spent putting it into operation. The declared objectives of the social revolution—for it is still going on—are Mexico for Mexicans, rights for the common man, and education for the common people —slogans which sound familiar to Anglo-Americans. In so radical a program vested interests have suffered. In the struggle the Church has been involved. Critics maintain that some of the reforms are more apparent than real; but the same has been said of other countries. Mexico is a dynamo of energy, a reservoir of wealth, a land of untold possibilities and of undoubted promise.

[46]

VII

Progress toward nationality in the Western Hemisphere has been attended by international adjustments. The interrelations of Canada and the United States have always been close, as their development has been in many ways parallel. Loyalists never forget their expulsion from the home hearth, nor the attempted conquest of 1812. Fortunately, as the Canadians say, the Americans were always just exasperating enough to prevent an international marriage, thus preserving Canadian nationality. By 1846 the old boundary questions had been settled. The mid-century was sometimes disturbed by annexation talk that was seldom dangerous. The war between the states and Fenian raids caused irritation. Fisheries and the Bering Sea were bones of contention. Blaine enjoyed twisting the British Lion's tail. Trade relations have sometimes been troublesome. But eventually these matters have been amicably settled. All in all, with common boundaries unfortified for more than a century, Canada and the United States, in this world of turmoil, furnish a splendid example of neighborliness.

Of the Hispanic republics the most intimate international contacts have been with each other. Like good Irishmen, whom they greatly resemble, the Latins quarrel among themselves but show solidarity against outsiders who interfere. Bullets often fly. But boundary disputes on many borders have been settled by arbitration, in which Latin America has set an example before the world. With Europe there has been occasional friction, but much more conspicuous has been the peaceful intercourse of commerce, investment, immigration, and cultural contacts.

Hispanic dealings with the United States have generally been closest in the adjacent regions; and by the rest of Latin America, naturally, these dealings have been taken as an index. Early friendships soon cooled. When the United States seized half of Mexico's domain, that country became embittered and other Latins suspicious. In the mid-century relations with Mexico greatly improved, and the long reign of Díaz was the heyday of American investors south of the Rio Grande. After the fall of "El General," the story was one of frequent intervention. Huerta was eliminated and Carranza elevated largely through Wilson's aid. Villa chasing and "saluting the flag" made Uncle Sam ridiculous. Mexico's new constitution threatened American investments and a decade of irritation followed. But this matter has been adjusted.[8] In recent years the United States has had its most intimate Latin American relations with the Isthmus and the Caribbean.

area, and there has exercised extensive supervisory functions. With South America, on the other hand, the tendency is toward recognition of the fullest autonomy. There the Monroe Doctrine is dead. The Southern Continent has grown up.[9]

The essential unity of the Western Hemisphere was revealed by the Great War. Every nation had to answer the question of participation or neutrality. Canada was in from the start; the United States moved more slowly. Until Uncle Sam joined the Allies, all Hispanic America held aloof. Then, of the twenty states to the south, eight joined the Allies, five broke all relations with Germany, and seven remained neutral. It is a significant thing that all America, from the north pole to the south pole, was either on the same side of the great struggle or remained neutral. There was emphatic Western Hemisphere solidarity.

The Americas have developed side by side. In the past their relations have been close; in the future they may or may not be closer. In the colonial period Latin greatly outweighed Saxon America. In the nineteenth century the balance tipped decisively in the other direction. But it is swinging back. The importance of Hispanic America as an economic unit and as a political factor is becoming greater from day to day. It is one of the great reservoirs of raw materials. It continues to attract foreign capital and foreign immigration. Saxon America, with its one hundred and forty millions of people, is practically closed to European settlers. Hispanic America, with its hundred millions, is wide open. A large German colony, it is reported, is right now being planned for the Upper Amazon—equipped with electric cooling plants and everything else up to date.[10] It is entirely possible that within a short time Hispanic will outnumber Saxon America, and with continued immigration its race stock will be more and more largely European. Ever since independence there has been fundamental Western Hemisphere solidarity. Therefore, it is not a matter of indifference to know that European influence in South America today far outweighs that of Saxon America, and that Europe is bending every effort to draw the Southern continent more and more into the European circle and away from its northern neighbors.

VIII

In this imperfect way I have endeavored to indicate some of the larger historical unities and interrelations of the Americas. Those outlined are only a few out of the many that are patent at every turn. Cultural and intellectual relations are quite as close and fully as important as political, territorial, and economic contacts. What I have said is intended merely as an illustration.

In recent years the range of investigation in Western Hemisphere history has vastly broadened. This is due in no small part to the influence of Jameson's guides to foreign archives; to the work of American and Canadian scholars on British America; of the students of the Caribbean; of the historians of the frontier; of the whole galaxy of Hispanists in many countries; of the social, economic, institutional, cultural, and diplomatic historians, the international relationists, and a host of others. Our historical data have not only become greater in amount but much more complex in character. Phases and factors formerly undreamed of have come to light. Many of the new discoveries do not fit into the nationalistic pattern. In the old synthesis their significance is lost. In a larger framework, on the other hand, many things which have seemed obscure and secondary become outstanding and primary.

This applies especially to borderland researches. Brebner studied the institutional relations of New England and the Maritime Provinces of Canada, and concluded that the histories of Canada and the United States should be treated as one. Just as emphatically, those who have studied borderland areas between Saxon and Hispanic America are convinced that the two fields are inextricably linked

[51]

together. Borderland zones are vital not only in the determination of international relations, but also in the development of culture. In this direction one of the important modifications of the Turner thesis is to be sought. By borderland areas not solely geographical regions are meant; borderline studies of many kinds are similarly fruitful.

It is not merely that a new framework will find a place for special researches that have already been consummated. Quite as important, a larger framework will call for data which we do not possess, and thus suggest a thousand new things to do. A classic example of the influence of a new synthesis is found in the multitude of investigators whom Turner set to work to fill out his elementary sketch. A report by a recent committee of historians complains that many doctoral thesis subjects in United States history have been cultivated past the point of diminishing returns. A larger synthesis of American history, I am sure, will do much to relieve this rather pathetic situation.[11] Who has written the history of the introduction of European plants and animals into the Western Hemisphere as a whole, or the spread of cattle and horse raising from Patagonia to Labrador? Who has written on a Western Hemisphere scale the history of shipbuilding and commerce, mining, Christian missions, Indian policies, slavery and emancipation, constitutional development, arbitration, the effects of the Indian on European cultures, the rise of the common man, or the development of art, architecture, literature, or science? Who has tried to state the significance of the frontier in terms of the Americas?

A noted historian has written for us the *Epic of America.* In his title "America" means the United States. We need an Adams to sketch the high lights and the significant developments of the Western Hemisphere as a whole. Perhaps the person who undertakes the task, as a guarantee of objectivity ought to be an inhabitant of the moon. But such a synthesis, done with similar brilliancy, would give us the "Epic of *Greater* America."

[1] This is so patent that it hardly needs demonstration, and for the future I foresee generally in practice two types of school and college courses in American history: an introductory, synthetic course, embracing the entire Western Hemisphere, analogous to courses in general European history; and courses in the history of the United States or of any other individual nation. In fact, a movement in this direction is well under way.

[2] England striped the Spanish Main (northern South America) with sea to sea grants which on the map look just as imposing as the more familiar grants in North America.

[3] Toronto, where this address was delivered.

[4] Brazil similarly seized Uruguay during the revolutionary disturbances, but relinquished it a few years later.

[5] It is interesting to note in passing that Samuel Hearne for the Hudson's Bay Company explored the Copper Mine country at the very same time that Daniel Boone reached the Mississippi. The two west moving columns were neck and neck.

[53]

[6] Across the river from the site of the present city of Portland.

[7] This is true of British, Dutch, and French America also.

[8] This adjustment did not prove to be permanent.

[9] The above was written in 1932.

[10] This colony did not materialize on any large scale.

[11] Before closing I wish to repeat with emphasis that I do not propose such a synthesis as a substitute for, but as a setting in which to place, any one of our national histories.

DEFENSIVE SPANISH EXPANSION
AND THE SIGNIFICANCE OF
THE BORDERLANDS *

I

The southern fringe of the United States was once an area lightly sprinkled with Spanish outposts and criss-crossed with Spanish trails. These Spanish Borderlands have had a picturesque, a romantic, and an important history. They had special significance as parts of the vast Spanish Empire, they are unique as the meeting place of two streams of European civilization, they have been potent factors in the interrelations between nations.

As parts of the Spanish Empire these borderlands have been sadly misunderstood in this country. They have been regarded as typical of Spanish America, and from this erroneous assumption false inferences have been drawn regarding Spain's part in the making of Western Hemisphere civilization.

* An Address delivered at the Boulder Conference on the History of the Trans-Mississippi West, June 18–21, 1929. Printed in *The Trans-Mississippi West,* edited by James F. Willard and Colin B. Goodykoontz. Boulder, University of Colorado, 1930.

It used to be the fashion to teach our children that Spain failed; that the Spaniards did not colonize but merely explored; that they killed off all the Indians; that the Spaniards were mere gold seekers, whereas the English came to America to found homes and build commonwealths, forgetting that gold seekers have been known to establish homes and build commonwealths.

This antithesis between the Spanish pick and the English hoe is after all somewhat fanciful and has been greatly overworked. A pioneer wrote: "There was no talke, no hope, nor worke, but dig gold. Such brute of gold, as one mad fellow desired to bee buried in the sandes, least they should by their art make gold of his bones." Surprisingly enough, this auriferous wail came not from one of Cortés' gold-seeking Spaniards, but from one of John Smith's Virginia home builders.

A grammar school text recently published by two very distinguished university professors contains the statement, inserted without visible sign of humor, that Spain did not colonize America, but merely tried to hold it to keep other nations out. The reason for such teaching is not far to seek. It was the inevitable result of writing United States history in isolation, apart from its setting in the history of the entire Western Hemisphere, of which the United States are but a part. It was the logical

[56]

corollary of restricting the study of American history to the region between the forty-ninth parallel and the Gulf of Mexico, as though that area were an inclusive and exclusive entity, and were synonymous with America.

With a vision limited by the Rio Grande, and noting that Spain's outposts within the area now embraced in the United States were slender, and that these fringes eventually fell into the hands of the Anglo-Americans, writers concluded that Spain did not really colonize, and that, after all, she failed. The fallacy came, of course, from mistaking the tail for the dog, and then leaving the dog out of the picture. The real Spanish America, the dog, lay between the Rio Grande and Buenos Aires. The part of the animal lying north of the Rio Grande was only the tail. Let us first glance at the dog.

II

America was the gift of Spain and Portugal to Europe. These nations followed the discovery with a brilliant era of exploration on sea and on land. In fifty years the sons of Iberia taught the world the most stupendous geography lesson it has ever had in any half century of recorded history. For this exploratory achievement Spain and Portugal have had their due meed of praise. But here appre-

ciation generally ends. Few realize that, compared
with their work of colonization, these epic explorations were but a minor part of what the two little
nations of the Peninsula contributed to the making
of the Western Hemisphere.

Surely, explorers did not build Mexico City and
Lima. Surely, wild-eyed gold seekers did not found
the universities of Mexico and Cordova. The old
nursery tale of mere explorers must have been a
myth, along with Santa Claus. Spain and Portugal
followed exploration by colonization. Only a small
fraction of their pioneers in America spent their
time running round the map. The vast majority
were merchants, planters, ranchers, soldiers, priests,
and miners. Settlement by them was so rapid, so
extensive, and so effective, that two-thirds of America are still Spanish and Portuguese today. The late
comers, France, Holland, England, and Russia,
found the ground preëmpted, and had to be content
with the left-over areas and the disputed borderlands to the north—the remaining one-third.

Spain's colonies expanded by a series of frontiers,
each with its own peculiar character, and each making its own contribution to American civilization.
The first step in the long and steady process was the
occupation of the West Indies. Here was the Mother
of America. Here Spain founded tropical plantations, a strategic outpost, a commercial focus, and

a base for expansion. Here she first coped with the difficult problem of native labor. Hither she transplanted the elements of her civilization before advancing to the mainland. Havana, Santo Domingo, and San Juan are symbols of the result. Columbus wrote from Isabella that although his men sickened and died, the sugar cane that he planted took root. The gigantic sugar interests of Cuba in 1932 are lineal descendants of the forty Spanish sugar mills that were being erected there in 1520.

South America was Spain's widest field of Western Hemisphere activity. From the islands, colonization advanced to the Isthmus, thence south to Peru. Here the conquest was followed by permanent settlement. Spanish institutions were set up —government, cities, haciendas, churches, monasteries, and schools. The University of Lima was founded in 1551. It was no great affair in the beginning, perhaps, but neither was Harvard ninety years later, when it graduated its first class of nine pupils of about high school grade. Lima became the metropolis of the Southern Continent.

Then came Peru's mining boom. Potosí, in upper Peru (now Bolivia), became the richest mining center in the world. In 1581 it had a population of 120,000, Moses tells us. Its wealth was astounding. This city alone spent $8,000,000 on the celebration of Philip II's accession to the throne (1556). A dead emperor was worth less than a live king. Nevertheless, three years later Potosí spent $140,000 on Charles V's funeral obsequies. Prior to 1593 the Potosí mines had paid the royal fifth on $396,000,-000 worth of silver. Nor was this status fleeting. Half a century later Potosí was still going strong, and in 1642 its citizens had $42,000,000 in cash and jewels tucked away in the local safe deposits.

Other South American areas tell a similar story. On the northern shoreline, the Spanish Main as the English called it, trading and pearl fishing stations grew into strong-walled cities. Cartagena was the home of San Pedro Claver, "sublime Apostle of the Negroes," and a forerunner of Wilberforce. Farther south, Bogotá became a center of culture which still prides itself on its literary taste and its pure Castilian speech and stock. It is enough to add that in Colombia the celebrated "Varones Illustres" was written in the sixteenth century, and that in Bogotá was operated the first astronomical observatory in America.

The conquest of Chile inspired and one of its conquerors wrote "La Araucana," one of the great epics of all literature of all time. Here the pioneers built Santiago, and made it a Pacific Coast center of industry and culture and the seat of an important university.

The La Plata Basin was somewhat slower to de-

velop, yet there also European civilization got a
permanent hold. Early efforts to colonize the mouth
of the great river were upset by the pull of Peru and
Paraguay. Colonists planted at Buenos Aires were
enticed away by the call of Bolivian silver. So Asun-
ción, a thousand miles inland, and not Buenos Aires,
became the first metropolis of the La Plata. Irala
the founder hastened the process by encouraging
intermarriage with the natives, setting a generous
example by taking unto himself seven daughters of
a powerful chief—potential oil queens they would
be now.

But the broad-bosomed river and the waving
pampas eventually had their way. Civilization reversed its course, and traveled down stream. Cordova, founded in a community of cowboys, became
the seat of a university that has been distinguished
ever since the seventeenth century. Buenos Aires,
refounded in 1580, came to stay, and to grow with
its nearly three million inhabitants into the Paris of
the Western Hemisphere.

The Portuguese had not been idle. The vast lit-
toral of Brazil was carved into feudal baronies
called *capitanías*. São Paulo, Pernambuco, Bahía
and Rio de Janeiro became nuclei of European
society in the sixteenth century. There, as in Spanish America, plantations, churches, monasteries,
schools, and colleges were built; there poets, his-

[61]

torians, and men of science lived and wrote. There were laid the foundations of what is now the second power in the Western Hemisphere.

In North America the Spanish pioneers were first attracted from the islands to the area occupied by the sedentary peoples. Mayas and Nahuas were brought under control, Spanish institutions were set up, and a large Spanish colony made this part of America their permanent home. Yes, Spaniards built homes. Alvarado's mansion, dating from 1524, is still a home of culture in Coyoacán. Cortés by his will declared himself an American, and ordered that his own bones and those of all his family should return to America for eternal rest.

Here as elsewhere the Spaniards built up more than they tore down. They fashioned churches, monasteries, and country mansions, on every hand. The University of Mexico was founded in 1551, simultaneously with that of Lima, and ere long its graduates were given postgraduate standing, without reduction of units or grade points, in the universities of Europe. Mexico City became the metropolis of European life and culture in all North America, a rank which it retained till near the end of the eighteenth century. In the days of the Inquisition and witch burning, not Mather of Boston, perhaps, but Sigüenza of Mexico City, was the first man of learning in the Western Hemisphere.

When the Englishman Thomas Gage visited the Aztec capital in the seventeenth century he was impressed by its wealth and refinement, and especially by the number of its coaches. In his book he tells us, "It is a byword that at Mexico there are four things fair, that is to say, the women, the apparel, the horses, and the streets. But to this I may add the beauty of some of the coaches of the Gentry, which do exceed in cost the best of the Court of Madrid and other parts of Christendom, for they spare no Silver, nor Gold, nor the best silks from China to enrich them. And to the gallantry of their horses the pride of some doth add the cost of bridles and shoes of silver." Indeed, "It was a most credible report that in Mexico in my time there were above fifteen thousand coaches," many, if not most of them, made in the same city.

Two decades were consumed in bringing Central America and southern Mexico under control. This was not primarily a period of mining, but of agricultural and commercial economy, based on the exploitation of native labor. Then great mineral veins were discovered in the central Mexican plateau. Mining rushes followed. Spanish gold was mainly silver, and millions of this metal poured into the royal treasury. It was these mines and those of South America that gave Charles V and Philip II their brilliant position in Europe. By the end of the sixteenth century all the great central plateau of Mexico had been colonized at strategic points. It was a mining society, and such it has remained in many of its essential characteristics to this day. There were "strikes," "rushes," and "boom towns," the prototypes of all later ones all the way from Mexico to Alaska. Mining camps became cities; the cities became the nuclei of new provinces, and now they are capitals of states. Zacatecas, Guanajuato, Durango, Saltillo, Mazapil and Monterrey, all founded in the sixteenth century, were not the work of mere explorers, but of permanent settlers and commonwealth builders, whose descendants still guide the destinies of the communities which these pioneers founded.

Beyond the mining frontier, in northern Mexico, settlement edged slowly forward in the decades that followed. In Coahuila, Chihuahua, and Sonora, miners, soldiers, missionaries, and cattlemen pushed their outposts just about to the present boundary between the United States and Mexico. With minor exceptions that boundary represents roughly the northern line of Spain's effective colonization.

Thus, by the end of the sixteenth century two-thirds of America has been staked out with permanent centers of Spanish and Portuguese life, and

[64]

this in the face of a mountain and desert geography which would have dismayed a people unused to mountains and deserts at home. This takes no account of areas explored, or of defensive salients that had been thrust out beyond the settled borders. The area then marked out for Hispanic America was almost the same as the area that is still Hispanic. What it lacked was added by the slow advance of the northern frontier in the seventeenth century, bringing the line of effective colonization up to the Rio Grande. The map of Hispanic America then was strikingly as it is today.

Within all that vast area, from El Paso to Buenos Aires, Hispanic American civilization continued to develop. Cities grew, commerce expanded, new mines were opened, herds grew larger, more plantations were tilled. By the end of the eighteenth century the Spanish population in America was three or four millions, and the Portuguese a million or more.[1]

And yet we say that Spain failed. But Spain and Portugal lost their colonies, someone reminds us. Yes, and so did England lose the best of hers. And the revolt of the colonies was the very best evidence of the real success of the mother countries in building up American commonwealths. Every worthwhile child, when he reaches majority, sets up for himself, or at least he makes clear his ability to do

[65]

so if he chooses. Anything else is a family tragedy. England raised up lusty children. Thirteen out of some thirty of them (not precisely the original thirteen) were vigorous enough to separate from the mother country and go it alone. The outcome was the United States. Spain and Portugal planted colonies, scattered over a vastly wider area than were England's children. They, too, became lusty. They, too, set up housekeeping for themselves. The outcome is a score of Hispanic American nations today. Washington and his associates merely started the American Revolution; Miranda, Bolívar, San Martín, Hidalgo, Morelos, and Iturbide carried it through. England's loss of her colonies was the real mark of her success as a colonizer. By the same token, Spain's loss of her colonies was the best evidence of her success in transplanting people and civilization. Greater Spain is over here, and what a proud old mother Spain should be. Greater Portugal is over here—Brazil—and what a proud little old mother Portugal should be. We even trust that Mother England does not look with disdain on her grown-up children over here.

III

So much for the dog; now for the tail. Away up here in the Far North, thousands of miles from the

Spanish centers at Mexico City, Guatemala, Bogotá, Santiago, and Buenos Aires, lay the northern fringes of the Spanish Empire—the northern borderlands. Outposts they were, but what a history they have had!

In the early years of the conquest this northern interior was a land of hope, concealing perhaps another Mexico or another Peru. It was a wonderland of romance, filled with figments of the imagination, suggested by misunderstood or jocose tales told by Indians who had a sense of humor, or who wished to pass their white visitors along.

On the Atlantic Coast, in the vast region called La Florida, there was the Fountain of Youth;[2] Cale, whose warriors wore golden helmets; Chicora, now Carolina, land of the giant King Datha. This monarch was not naturally monstrous, but in his youth he merely had been rubbed with grease and stretched. In his kingdom, too, there was a species of deer which generously fed the inhabitants on milk, thus absolving them from the primal curse of labor. There was the Queen of Cufitachiqui, land of pearls. Somewhere in the South Carolina Piedmont there was fabulous Diamond Mountain, and if you didn't believe it you could ask Sir Francis Drake.

In the west lay Gran Quivira, land whose ruler was lulled to sleep by golden bells, and whose bor-

[67]

ders were bathed by a stream in which swam fish as big as horses. Near Quivira lay Gran Teguayo and the Kingdom of the Texas. Still farther west were the Seven Cities of Cíbola, whose many-storied towns had turquoise-studded doors. Somewhere beyond the Colorado were people who lived under water; another tribe who sat in the shade of their own generous-sized ears; and still other people who did not eat their food, but lived on smells. Finally, on the western coast there were islands bearing pearls, and another whose only metal was gold; there was the Amazon Queen, the California lady with the enormous feet; and, last of these western "monstrosities," as the chronicler called them, a race of bald-headed men. Bald heads were the limit. Father Escobar, to whom the Indian wag recounted these wonders of the West, had a lovable human urge to believe in them. Wrong-headed persons might doubt such tales, he said, but, he reminded all such, "for anyone who will consider the wonders which God constantly does perform in this world, it will be easy to believe that since he is able to create these monstrosities he may have done so."

Then there were geographical notions, the offspring of a desire to get quickly to India. America tapered down toward the north like an inverted radish and brought the oceans close together. From the St. Lawrence River, or from Chesapeake Bay, a strait led to a great inland sea, or better, from ocean to ocean. Somewhere west of the upper Rio Grande the desert concealed a lake of gold, fabulous turquoise mines, and the smoke-hued Sierra Azul. And there was the north branch of the Colorado River, a second outlet, which, turning west across Nevada, merrily threaded its way through the high Sierras of California, and meandered to the ocean somewhere near San Francisco Bay.

So long as they remained untested by hard and disappointing experience, all these wonders were incentives to heroic endeavor. It was to pierce this Northern Mystery and prove these tales that epic jaunts were made by eager-eyed adventurers. Under other names, these borderlands had their Columbus, their Lindbergh, their Commander Byrd. This was "earth's high holiday." Romance was here.

> He does not guess, the quiet-eyed
> As he goes by in his young pride,
> Who rode beside! Who rode beside!

Not alone Lancelot, and Galahad, and Arthur, and the Maid, rode beside Lindbergh that day in May two years ago. With him were Narváez, De Soto, Cabrillo and Coronado, too, and many another "who dared his own wild dreams to try" in these Spanish Borderlands.

Like apparitions, Narváez and De Soto flitted through the vast region called La Florida, only to find watery graves. Coronado sought wealth and fame in Gran Quivira, and returned to Mexico a broken man. Cabrillo, trusting his fate to the South Sea waves, was lured to his death by the California Lorelei. These bold adventurers gained little wealth, but their heroic marches were by no means idle jaunts or wild-goose chases. They quieted for a time the extravagant tales of great cities in the north, and taught Europe an important lesson in American geography. Each tortuous line which they left on the sixteenth century map stands for some rumor run to its lair. Twenty years of trial put most of the yarns to rest for the nonce, and the adventurers settled back on the established frontier.

Sixteenth century Spanish expansion, with minor exceptions, had been mainly economic and missionary in its urge. Settled Indians to exploit and convert, tropical plantations, mines, stock ranches, and commerce had been the lodestones leading to new frontiers. But already another factor had entered into the process—a force which became increasingly important with the passage of time until it became a primary motive to further Spanish advance to new areas. This factor was defence. With the exception of New Mexico, Spanish coloniza-in the northern borderlands was chiefly defensive

[70]

in its origin. In the advance into these regions missionary work was always conspicuous and important. But in the order of urgency, missions here occupied a second place, and were a means to the primary end.

IV

The rest of Europe looked with envious eyes on Spain's monopoly in the Western Hemisphere, and registered protests. In South America Spain suffered the persistent inroads of the Portuguese from Brazil. Papal bulls and a treaty established a Line of Demarcation. Brazilian slave hunters snapped their fingers at both Pope and treaty. They raided Indian villages beyond the line, and drove back chain gangs of captives for the sugar plantations. Jesuit missionaries were sent to hold the outraged Spanish border. In reply the Brazilians stormed defenseless missions and carried off trembling neophytes. Behind these Mameluke slavers Portuguese settlers followed. On the Brazilian border Spain's frontiers gradually yielded. The Line of Demarcation was sadly bent, until it came to resemble a bow, with the old papal line as the string. And so it stands today.

On her northernmost borders Spain suffered the onslaughts of French, Dutch, English, and Russians, not all at once, but in successive clashes. Most of her expansive energy north of the Gulf and the Rio Grande was expended to meet these incursions. One by one, as occasion required, defensive salients were thrust out, like men moved forward on a checkerboard to counter the plays of an aggressive opponent.

Economic in its origin, Spain's Caribbean outpost became more and more defensive. French, English, and Dutch pirates raided treasure fleets and sacked towns. Spain replied by building walls around her coast cities, and policing the Caribbean with a naval fleet—the Armada de Barlovento.

Fifty years of prospecting and rainbow chasing in La Florida (the Atlantic mainland) proved profitless to promoters and painful to many broken heads. Philip had just decided to leave La Florida to hostile Creeks and hellish hurricanes, when French intrusion forced his hand. Ribaut occupied Port Royal, and Laudonnière settled near the site of Jacksonville. Now came Menéndez with a will strong enough to destroy the French, and a force adequate to defend the threatened coast. The awful slaughter at the French fort has echoed to the twentieth century. But the Peninsula was permanently occupied, Spanish outposts of defence were thrust up the coast to Port Royal, and momentarily even to Chesapeake Bay.

The New Mexico salient was only partially defensive in origin, but it was foreign danger that finally nerved Spain to take the deep plunge into the distant wilderness. Coronado found Cíbola disappointing. What to Friar Marcos had appeared a jeweled city, looked through the soldier's gold-tinged spectacles like a crowded little village "crumpled all up together." Cíbola yielded no gold, the conqueror had a young bride at home, so to Mexico he returned. But time and distance encouraged new flights of fancy. From the resemblance of the Pueblos to the Aztec dwellings the region came to be called New Mexico. It was after all the "Otro México" which so many had sought. There were settled Indians to convert, and foreign danger lurked in the background. Beyond the Pueblos lay the Strait of Anián, whose western extremity the pirate Drake was supposed to have found. New Mexico therefore offered an opportunity to spread the Faith, exploit Indian labor, and protect the Empire. Ten years were spent in indecision. The defeat of the Armada gave the final scare, and New Mexico was colonized.

Now, like an athlete, gathering force for a mighty spring, the frontier of settlement leaped eight hundred miles into the wilderness, from southern Chihuahua to the Upper Rio Grande. Thither Oñate led his colony with paternal care.

[73]

Eighty wagons creaked their lumbering way across the grim, wide desert, and seven thousand head of stock kicked up the dust over the trail several miles wide. In the narrow but well-watered Rio Grande Valley the colonists settled among the Pueblo Indians. Friars built missions, soldiers warded off attacks of relentless Apaches, and civilians founded a semi-pastoral society. For two hundred and fifty years Santa Fé stood like a sentinel on the very rim of European civilization.

Another foreign head to crack popped up on the Texas horizon. Eager Franciscans, looking across the Rio Grande at the great "Kingdom of the Texas," had urged the king on. But he had no funds. Why must Spain be hurried? She was on the way; give her time and she would arrive. Ten thousand miles of actual settlements already gave her quite enough trouble and care. Then La Salle's colony intruded. Presto! Carlos roused himself, found money in another pocket, and hurried soldiers and missionaries to the border to hold the threatened land. Massanet, devout friar, and De León, seasoned Indian fighter, joined hands in defence of the realm. The French danger momentarily subsided and Texas was abandoned, only to be reoccupied when France founded Louisiana and split the Spanish Borderlands in two. Now a stronger colony was sent to the eastern Piney

Woods. Los Adaes became the outpost against the French at Natchitoches. San Antonio, planted as a half-way base, became a superb missionary center, where no less than nine missions sooner or later dotted the banks of the one little San Antonio River.

For half a century Los Adaes guarded the French border; then Louisiana was ceded to Spain. There was no French danger now. "Todos somos Españoles," De Mézières told the Indians. "We are now all Spaniards." Forthwith, soldiers and missionaries, by government fiat, abandoned the border, though a few colonists held on. San Antonio, Nacogdoches, and lesser settlements had taken root and they continued to survive. These defensive outposts had held Texas for Spain against French inroads, and they made Jefferson's later claim to Texas as a part of Louisiana historically unsound.

The Louisiana cession hurled Spain from the frying pan into the fire. A small ill on the Red River was swapped for a mortal danger on the Mississippi. France had long held the Great Valley. But now the Lily came down before the Union Jack. With Canada the eastern half of the Valley went to Britain, but the western half was ceded to Spain to save it from a similar fate. To Carlos III, the energetic Spanish king, the gift looked like a White Elephant. What could Spain do with it? With settlements extending from Santa Fé to Buenos Aires

[75]

she was already land poor. But arguments had no weight in the case. Louisiana, like another baby, had arrived, and must be cared for. Spain must occupy the province or the oncoming English would seize it. They had invaded Georgia and made their title good by force. In the late war they had taken Florida, too. Their buckskin-shirted pioneers were pushing over the Alleghanies, and even crossing the Father of Waters. Soon they would invade Texas, and endanger the heart of Mexico. Perhaps not all these advancing frontiersmen were quite so fear-inspiring as Mike Fink. This boastful specimen said of himself, "I can outrun, outhop, throw down, drag out, and lick any man in the country. I'm a Salt River Roarer, I am. I love the Wimming, and I'm chock full of fight."

So, reluctantly Carlos III took hold of the vast region called Louisiana, before too many Mike Finks should arrive. The French inhabitants, mourning the old flag, started a revolution, but Don Alejandro O'Reilly gave his firing squad a little target practice and Spain was in the saddle. The East Texas military frontier was now abandoned. Defence was concentrated on the Mississippi, and soon there was a line of posts extending from New Orleans to St. Louis.

Louisiana was not Charles III's only frontier problem. Simultaneously another arose on the Pa-

cific Coast. Spain had long talked of advancing
her settlements to Alta California. Lower California and Pimería Alta (southern Arizona) had
been occupied at the end of the seventeenth century. Vizcaíno had chased elk in Carmel Valley and
boosted the "fine harbor of Monterey." Zealous
friars painted in glowing colors the missionary field
awaiting them in the populous towns along the
Santa Barbara Channel. If only the king would
help, what a harvest they would reap! But there was
a vast desert gap to cross, and the king always had
more pressing tasks in other corners of the hemisphere. So California waited until an emergency
should arise.

That emergency came when Russia threatened
to extend her settlements from Alaska down the
Pacific Coast. Carlos III was not a man who tem-
porized, and he proceeded to occupy Alta California. Square-jawed Gálvez organized the expedition. Its immediate purpose was to hold the harbor
of Monterey, for the Golden Gate and San Francisco Bay had not yet been discovered. In command
of the enterprise went Portolá. At the head of the
immortal missionary band was Junípero Serra, a
man remarkable among all pioneers in American
history.

With vigor the plan was put into execution. San
Diego was occupied as a half-way base in the sum-

mer of 1769; a year later the flag of Spain floated over Monterey Bay. Between these two strategic points a celebrated chain of missions was begun. Meanwhile Portolá discovered the Golden Gate and San Francisco Bay. Anza now opened a land route from Sonora, and a year later, in a superb feat of frontiering, he led over the same trail a colony of two hundred and forty persons to found San Francisco, on what Father Font, the diarist, called "that prodigy of nature . . . the harbor of harbors."

The Russian threat had forced the Spanish frontier one long notch higher; the ubiquitous English now gave it another hoist. British traders began to swarm the waters of the North Pacific. Thereupon Spain extended California even to Nootka Sound (now in British Columbia), establishing there a slender presidio and a little mission. But England shook her fist, the cards were stacked against Spain, and she withdrew to San Francisco.

Outposts so scattered called for lines of communication. Men who dared were not lacking, and Spain's frontiersmen, under the direction of the great viceroy Bucareli, proceeded to tie the border provinces together. The pathfinding energy displayed in the last quarter of the eighteenth century was scarcely less vigorous than that of the golden days of the sixteenth. Level-headed Anza had

opened a route from Sonora to California. Santa Fé
now became the hub of long exploratory spokes
thrust forth to connect the new outposts with the
old. Fearless Garcés, prince of lonely wanderers,
showed a way from Santa Fé to Los Angeles. Escalante, on a similar mission, made his prodigious
odyssey of two thousand miles from Santa Fé
through Colorado, Utah, and Arizona and back to
Santa Fé. De Mézières, Vial, and their associates,
blazed communication lines connecting Santa Fé
with San Antonio, Natchitoches, and St. Louis.
Finally, in an effort to connect Louisiana with
Spain's Nootka settlement, men sent out from St.
Louis ascended the Missouri River as far as the
Yellowstone.

Santa Fé became more than ever a strategic outpost, but now chiefly against the Indians. Compe-
tent Anza, called to hold the New Mexico border,
ascended San Luis Valley, descended the Arkansas
River, somewhere in the Greenhorn Mountains met
the valiant Comanche chief Cuerno Verde (hence
the name Greenhorn), and proved himself to be
one of the best Indian fighters who ever battled in
Colorado.

Anyone who proposes to talk of Spain's deca-
dence in the eighteenth century should first study
the superb corps of men operating in her northern
provinces and the defensive program which they

[79]

carried through with slender resources after the Seven Years' War.

V

All these salients—La Florida, Texas, Louisiana, and California—in origin were defensive outposts, and so they were regarded by Spain. To hold them she utilized especially her two typical frontier institutions, the presidio and the mission.

The presidio was a soldier garrison. It might be composed of ten men or of two hundred, according to the need. Its function was to give military protection to its district, sending out detachments here, there, and yonder, scouting, chasing Indians, ejecting intruders. Temporary garrisons might occupy the merest shacks. Important and permanent presidios were provided with fortifications. The most substantial of all the northern line was the one at St. Augustine. Presidios, temporary or permanent, were scattered all along the frontier of New Spain. Port Royal, San Agustín, Apalache, Pensacola, New Orleans, the Arkansas Post, St. Louis, Natchitoches, Los Adaes, San Antonio, La Bahía, San Sabá, San Juan Bautista, Ojinaga, El Paso, Santa Fé, Janos, Tubac, Tucson, Altar, and the four in Alta California—San Diego, Santa Barbara, Monterey, and San Francisco—were the more notable of the presidios of the northern borderlands. But numerous other points, all the way from Georgia to San Francisco were occupied for longer or shorter periods, as occasion demanded.

Beside the presidial soldier went the missionary. The mission was par excellence a frontier institution. The missionary was an agent not only of the Church, but of the State as well. His primary business was to save souls and spread Spanish civilization among the heathen. The heathen were to be found on the frontier, beyond the established settlements. Here was the missionary's proper field of endeavor. As soon as his pioneer work among the Indians on one frontier was done, he was expected to turn his flock over to the parish clergy and move on to a new tribe, farther in the wilderness.

Theoretically at least, the State was just as anxious as the Church to Christianize and civilize the heathen. But it cost money to run Indian schools (for such the missions were) and the king's money had to be spent where it was most needed. The missionary field was unlimited, and the friars were always pulling at the rein. Not all the demands made on the royal treasury could be satisfied, and those most urgent first got attention. On the frontiers endangered by foreign foes there was a double need. Soldiers sent there could both keep out Europeans and protect the missions. Many times the sovereigns had

[81]

to turn deaf ears to missionary appeals for funds and permission to go to work among outlying tribes. But when political danger coincided with missionary opportunity, the friars had their way. Then they went beside the soldier to help hold the endangered frontier for Spain, at the same time that they saved souls and spread Spanish civilization.

In fact, the friars often cleverly turned foreign danger to their own account. They saw on some international border a tribe outside the Christian fold. They begged for funds and permission to go. Neither was forthcoming. Then a rumor was heard of impending foreign aggression. Stationed on the frontier, and first to hear the rumors, the friars reported them to the viceroy. They wielded good pens and their words carried weight. The outcome, often, was a new defensive advance of soldier and missionary, to hold the border against a threatening European neighbor.

Father Hidalgo was a good example. He had been in East Texas, but with the rest of the friars had retreated to the Rio Grande. His heart yearned for his Texans. Again and again he begged for permission to return to them, but his superiors refused. Then the French played into his hands. They had founded Louisiana. If he could wave a French flag before the viceroy's eyes things would move. So he wrote a cryptic letter to the missionaries of Louisiana. It fell into the hands of Cadillac, the governor. Cadillac wanted trade with the Spaniards, and here was a chance. So he sent St. Denis, his ablest frontiersman, to confer with Father Hidalgo, and see what he could see. St. Denis crossed Louisiana and Texas, traveling nearly a thousand miles, to find the friar. When he reached the Rio Grande Hidalgo had returned to Mexico. But his associates there saw the significance of what had happened. Three of them wrote him in words to the same effect:

"Albricias, Padre! Reward me for great news! The French are here! Now your dream will come true! Now you will be sent back to your beloved Texans." And sent he was. It was now that East Texas was permanently occupied to keep back the French, and Father Hidalgo was among the defenders of the border.

The soldier and the missionary were the primary agencies by which defensive expansion was effected. It was all the better if civil settlers could be had, to supplement the work of the leather-jacket and the friar. So small civil colonies generally were added. Such a colony went to San Agustín, one to Santa Fé, another to San Antonio, and still others to California. The presidio and mission became nuclei around which ranchers settled on generous land grants. Re-

[83]

tired presidial soldiers generally became settlers in the vicinity of their posts. Roman history was repeated here.

So these slender defensive and missionary outposts took root in the soil. As a result, nearly every stable presidio, and many missions, slowly grew into permanent settlements. Most of the old Spanish towns along the frontier, like St. Augustine, San Antonio, Tucson, San Diego, Los Angeles, Santa Barbara, Monterey, and San Francisco have grown from small beginnings as presidios or missions or both.

Such in brief were these northern borderlands, as viewed from the standpoint of the Spanish Empire. In Madrid, in Lima, in Buenos Aires, in Mexico, they were regarded as defensive and missionary fringes. The real Spanish America lay to the south of them.

VI

Having established these defensive salients, Spain was put to it to retain them. International in origin, they continued to be international in significance. As the English frontier moved westward, the Anglo-Spanish borders overlapped in a succession of areas, and one by one a series of conflicts resulted—in the Caribbean, in Georgia and Florida, in Louisiana, in Texas, in New Mexico, in California. The Anglo-American advance stopped in each case when it reached the line of effective Spanish colonization. It was the borderlands mainly which Spain lost to England and the United States. We have witnessed Spain's rising tide on the border; we may now follow it as it ebbs. I hold no brief for any side in the long series of contests. To the historian it is not a matter of right and wrong, but just a human tale. His business is to watch and try to understand the drama.

On the Caribbean fringe the English colonized some of Spain's neglected islands, and conquered Jamaica. To the English at Charleston, Guale (Spanish Georgia) was a challenge. Finding themselves "in the very chaps of the Spaniards," they proceeded on the motto, "Guale delenda est." The Mamelucos of Brazil were emulated now by the Carolina hunters of Indian slaves. They destroyed the missions and carried off the neophytes to work on plantations. Ex-governor Moore in one campaign destroyed thirteen Apalache missions, burned several captives at the stake, and took away fourteen hundred neophytes as prisoners. Oglethorpe's Georgia Colony was founded more as a buffer against the Spaniards than as a philanthropic enterprise. Spain contested these inroads, but in the Seven Years' War she was forced to give way, losing both Georgia and Florida.

At the same time, by the gift of Louisiana, Spain acquired a long frontage against the English on the Mississippi. Anglo-Americans now poured over the mountains into Kentucky and Tennessee. In the Floridas British traders, like Lachlan McGillivray, married the dusky daughters, and thus cemented their hold on the tribes. Little checked by the legal boundary, long-hunters and horse drovers began to cross into Louisiana.

During the Revolution Spain aided the American colonies against England and recovered Florida, much reduced now by the loss of the Georgia part, but increased by the scrap of old French territory which England had erected into West Florida.

By aiding the American Revolution, Spain had hastened the growth of an aggressive neighbor. Through her recovery of the Floridas, she had merely increased her burdens, by lengthening the line which she must defend. All the way from Amelia Island to Minnesota now the Anglo-Americans intruded. Having recovered Florida, Spain essayed to maintain its extreme boundaries. She denied the validity of a treaty to which she was not a party. She utilized British traders to offset the Yankees. She closed the Mississippi to American commerce. She entered into intrigues with Kentuckians and Tennesseeans, offering trade in return for favors. She established a garrison in the Chick-

[86]

asaw country to hold the line of the Tennessee. She tried building up a buffer state, by counter-colonizing Florida and Louisiana, even coaxing in Americans, in the vain hope that they would hold back their brothers and cousins. But it was all to no avail. Spain was operating too far from her base, and in the Pinckney treaty she finally yielded the disputed area.

It is absurd to regard the outcome of this contest as merely an index of the relative strength of two civilizations, as some have done. It reveals rather the advantage of an expanding economic frontier working from an immediate base, over a defensive frontier operating a long distance from the centers of resources and population. The Anglo-American lever had a long power arm and a short weight arm; the Spanish government operated with the weight too far from the fulcrum. If the interests at stake and the distances of the contested area from the population centers had been reversed, the story would perhaps have been different.

Now the shadow of the Corsican crept over the Mississippi Valley. Napoleon unceremoniously took Louisiana out of Spanish hands. Spain was humiliated, of course, but at Madrid there was a sigh of relief at the thought of letting France be the buffer against the Frankenstein which Spain had helped to bring into existence. Then Fortune took a new turn. Instead of taking charge of Louisiana himself, Napoleon sold it to the United States. The Little Corporal, for his own purposes, had pushed the Anglo-American frontier one long notch nearer to the heart of Mexico.

Doggedly Spain held on. She had colonized Texas in the eighteenth century to keep out the French. She now recolonized it to restrain the more feared Americans. Adaes, the old Texas capital, was reoccupied. Garrisons or small colonies were distributed along the Camino Real from San Antonio to Adaes, on the Lower Trinity, and on the Gulf Coast. From San Antonio and from Santa Fé scouting parties went forth to work with renewed vigor among the Indians of the plains, to hold them in line against the oncoming Gringoes. Jefferson's Red River explorers were driven back. Melgares rode across the prairies and defiantly ran up the Spanish flag at a Pawnee village. Withdrawing with Fabian tactics, he welcomed Pike at Santa Fé and took him a prisoner to Chihuahua.

Spain stubbornly contested Jefferson's boundary claims. The American president cast his eye over the map. Then, on every uncertain border he loyally gave his own country the benefit of the doubt. He claimed West Florida as a part of old French Louisiana, which it was; he claimed Texas as a part of old French Louisiana, which it was not, for

Spain had occupied it for over a century. Jefferson even suggested that the Oregon Country might be a part of Louisiana. Such a contention could do no harm.

Diplomatic jousts followed. Napoleon was appealed to, but he refused to browbeat Spain into acquiescence in American demands. A little war on the Texas border shaved off a small slice of Spanish territory between Adaes and the Sabine River.

Then opportunity knocked at the American door. Spain's colonies rose in revolt. Hidalgo gave the *Grito de Dolores.* All the way from Buenos Aires to Baton Rouge the flame of revolution raged. Democracy's blood was stirred in the neighbor republic. Here was a mission. It would be glorious to spread liberty into a king-ruled country. Out of the mouths of Drake and Cromwell, English and Americans had learned to talk of "Spanish tyranny." (The "Devildoms of Spain" was a later inspiration to Tennyson.) There were old scores to settle. There were boundary disputes, and Spain's restrictive system made commerce with her colonies possible only by contraband. American smugglers on the Spanish borders, all the way from San Agustín to Santa Fé, and all round the rim of South America, had been thrown into Spanish dungeons.

Here was a chance. English, Irish, Scotch, Latin and nondescript Americans, encouraged by the

President of the United States, in the name of liberty set up a Lone Star Republic in West Florida and an ill-starred one in East Florida. Then Madison seized West Florida to keep order and forestall England. The Grito de Dolores was echoed at San Antonio. Freedom-loving, adventure-loving, land-hungry Americans raised an army of liberation, swept Texas, and gave their lives at the Battle of the Medina.

In East Florida British influence continued. Americans encroached on Indian lands, and border troubles increased. So Jackson went in with an army. Spain, in trouble at home, her colonies in North and South America in revolt, was helpless to resist. Seeing her other colonies going, and both Floridas virtually lost, she took a price for the latter and legalized the title of the United States. The so-called Florida Purchase was quite as much an incident in the Spanish-American Guerra de la Independencia as in the Anglo-American territorial expansion.

All this long border struggle availed Spain little for her immediate ends. The Wars of Independence succeeded. By 1822 most of South America, and all of Spanish North America to Red River and the forty-second parallel, had won their independence.

The drama was now shifted from Spain to Mexico and to the region beyond Red River and the

roof of the Rockies. Here the old Spanish Borderlands continued to play a leading part in inter-
American relations, and more than ever they
became a meeting place of two European civilizations. Mexico, less exclusive than Spain, opened a
field for freer action. The thrilling tale of southwestern diplomacy, politics, and war has oft been
told. I must limit myself here mainly to race contacts and enduring survivals.

VII

These southwestern lands had long been a mag-
net to adventure and trade. The very presence of
Spanish settlements rather increased than checked
the inquisitiveness of Spain's neighbors. In this way
they were a cause of the very ill which they were
designed to cure.

Even in early French days the Spanish outposts
greatly accelerated the advance of the explorer's
and trader's frontier. Everywhere in French America there were rumors of Spanish mines in the distant Southwest. Spain would be mistress of the
Pacific and keep it a closed Spanish lake. She for-
got that the surest way to spread the news in this old
world was to whisper "Don't tell anybody." The
very air of mystery bred exaggerated notions of
Spanish wealth and piqued the Canadian's curios-

ity. So Frenchmen were drawn like flies to the Spanish borderlands. Having attracted them, Spain found difficulty in keeping them out.

Records tell of French treasure hunters way out on the New Mexico border before the end of the sixteenth century, long before Quebec was founded. From the days of Joliet and Marquette *coureurs de bois* crossed the Mississippi and headed toward Santa Fé and Coahuila. La Salle has usually been pictured as the great defender of the French against the advancing English, but he was quite as much concerned with the Spanish border far to the southwest. A prominent part of his western plan was to establish a French base on the Gulf of Mexico from which to conquer the Chihuahua mines and open a French highway across Mexico to the Pacific. The Spanish settlements became the principal source for the French supply of horses, and from La Salle's day forward Frenchmen were drawn to the Spanish outposts, or to the Indian tribes between, to get droves of mounts for Illinois and even for Canada. In the eighteenth century, long before the Louisiana cession to Spain, there was a veritable outburst of French energy directed toward finding a way to Santa Fé with a view to trade and prospect for mines. Several parties besides the well-known Mallet brothers succeeded in reaching their goal.

So it was with the Anglo-Americans. As they

moved westward step by step from the Atlantic seaboard, they always had on their left flank a Spanish neighbor. This very Spanish presence, whether distant or less remote, was a stimulus to adventure. The Southwest was the abiding place of Romance. Red-blooded Anglo-American youth, seeking the coquettish lady, hoped to find her at the end of the trail leading to Nacogdoches, to San Antonio, to Santa Fé, to Los Angeles. Returning heroes claimed to have found her. They told of dark-eyed señoritas, and of an exotic life in a foreign land, for such it was.

James Ohio Pattie, prince of braggarts, had scarcely reached New Mexico when he heroically rescued from murderous Indians the beautiful Jacova, daughter of the governor. The señorita did her part by falling head over heels in love with her gallant benefactor—so the modest Pattie tells us. Ruxton wrote a book intended to astonish stay-at-homes with the mighty deeds of the American Mountain Men. There was fandango at Taos, that gateway to New Mexico. The American beaux captured not only all the señoritas, but the señoras as well. The jealous caballeros pulled their knives. Kit Carson to the rescue! He seizes a three-legged stool, rends it limb from limb, distributes the legs, and with them, he, Dick Wootton, and La Bonté clear the room of all but the Americans and the

[93]

clinging señoritas. "That's the place for me," rang
the chorus back East, when hot-blooded Youth read
the tale.

Official explorations to the southwestern border
were likewise hastened by the presence of foreign
settlements in a coveted land. Pike was sent quite as
much to take a peep at New Mexico as to get topo-
graphical information about Colorado, or to put
his name on Pike's Peak. Jefferson, when he sent
Freeman, Hunter, and Dunbar to explore Red
River, was probably more interested in Natchitoches than in Red River Raft.

Southwestern trade was hastened by the presence
of the Spanish settlements. On some frontiers there
were none but Indians with whom to dicker. In the
Southwest there were Spaniards, too. If commerce
could be only clandestine, the challenge merely
piqued the more. Way back in the eighteenth century Anglo-Americans took up the southwestern
horse and mule trade. Before the Revolution, Vir-
ginians, among them Governor Patrick Henry, obtained Spanish horses through the Pawnee Indians,
or bought better stock directly from the Spanish
provinces. Daniel Boone, falling for a moment from
his high estate as long-hunter and scout, once at least
gave "bar" and Indian "varmint" a respite while he
conducted a drove of Spanish horses from Louisiana to Georgia. Philip Nolan, commonly called

[94]

filibuster, was primarily horse drover, operating between the Rio Grande and the American settlements east of the Mississippi. Sometimes the stock driven by these traders was legally purchased, sometimes it was captured wild; quite as often it was stolen from the Spaniards by Indian middlemen, or by the traders themselves.

Long-haired Americans covered wide spaces to smuggle merchandise into New Orleans, San Antonio, and Saltillo. Santa Fé was an objective to traders long before the uninhabited stretches lying between it and St. Louis. Pike, released from Chihuahua, was a returned Marco Polo, and more than one trader's hand was made to itch by his tale of New Mexico's enticing commerce, and more than one mouth to water when he wrote of El Paso's thrifty vineyards, and "the finest wine ever drank in the country—celebrated through all the provinces." The great Santa Fé Trail was beaten wide and deep by tobacco-chewing Missourians bound for Taos, Santa Fé, Chihuahua, and Los Angeles, because there lived señoritas who coveted calicoes, and caballeros who could pay for them in mules or silver dollars.

VIII

Accelerated adventure, exploration, and trade in the Spanish Borderlands meant an acceleration of settlement. Behind it was the mighty push of American growth. The outcome was inevitable. The vanguard spied out the land and to them it seemed good. Trappers from the hard mountain wilderness found Taos and Santa Fé comfortable places in which to settle down. To the men with Jedediah Smith, who had crossed the dreary deserts of Utah and Nevada to California, Mission San Gabriel looked like the Promised Land, and Rogers, who wrote the diary, could not have smacked his lips with greater gusto at manna from Heaven than he did at the welcoming glass of "good old whiskey," and the "dinner of fish and fowl, beans, potatoes—grapes as dessert, wine, gin, and water plenty" with which he was served by the Spaniards who, though "catholicks by profession," appeared to be "gentlemen of the first class," and who surprised the good Presbyterian by allowing him full "liberty of conscience," and even patiently indulged him while he, without the flicker of a smile, tried to correct their theology and to save their souls.

No wonder that many trappers and traders remained to settle. They had found a pleasant berth. The first comers were imperceptibly absorbed into the Spanish communities. Most of the vanguard married in the country and became members of old families. We find such on every border, in Florida, in Louisiana, in Texas, in New Mexico, in Arizona.

In California, long before the Mexican War, it was a customary boast of a señorita that she would marry a blue-eyed man. Hundreds made good their vow, and before the American flag arrived nearly every California town had one or more American settlers married to heiresses, with whom they acquired landed estates. It was a story not unlike that of Oklahoma in more recent times—the landed heiress then becomes the oil queen now. Florida, Louisiana, Texas, New Mexico, and California all had their influential Anglo-American settlers while the land was still a part of Spain or Mexico. Florida had her Alexander McGillivray, William Panton, and William Augustus Bowles; Louisiana, her Oliver Pollock, Daniel Clark, Philip Nolan, Daniel Boone, and Moses Austin; New Mexico, her Bents and her Kit Carson; Texas, her Edward Murphy, Samuel Davenport, James Dill, William Barr, and Jim Bowie; California, her Abel Stearns, John A. Sutter, Henry Fitch, and Thomas O. Larkin.

These early comers to the borderlands found the back breaking work of pioneering already done for them. Between 1841 and the Gold Rush no less than fifteen organized caravans of overland immigrants entered California to settle. They could hardly be called pioneers. They entered an established community. Although trespassers, they were given a

[97]

friendly welcome. They readily obtained supplies at the missions, ranches, and towns, and often found employment to tide them over until they were permanently established. Even the Forty-niners found the Spanish ranches an important source of supply. In Texas the American migration after 1820 was so large and so rapid that it could not be thus absorbed, and in California, during the Gold Rush, the native population was soon swamped by the invading host. But New Mexico is even yet a community that is nearly half Spanish.

Thus it is that the old Spanish Borderlands were the meeting place and fusing place of two streams of European civilization, one coming from the south, the other from the north.

IX

Slender though these Spanish outposts were, they left their mark deep on the land. The rule of Spain has passed; but her colonies have grown into independent nations. From Mexico to Chile, throughout nearly half of the Western Hemisphere, the Spanish language and Spanish institutions are still dominant. Even in the old borderland north of the Rio Grande and the Gulf, the imprint of Spain's sway is still deep and clear. The Anglo-American commonwealths that are their heirs have

received from them a heritage with which they
would not willingly part. The names of four States
—Florida, Colorado, Nevada, and California—are
Spanish in form. Scores of rivers and mountains,
and other scores of town and cities in the southern
United States, still bear the names of saints dear to
the Spanish pioneers. Southwestern Indians yet
speak Spanish in preference to English. Many
towns have Spanish quarters, where the life of the
old days still goes on, and where one can always
hear the soft Castilian tongue. Southwestern English has been enriched by Spanish contact, and hundreds of words of Spanish origin are in current use
in speech and print everywhere along the border.

Throughout these Hispanic regions now in Anglo-
American hands, Spanish architecture is conspicuous. Scattered all the way from Georgia to San
Francisco are the ruins of Spanish missions. Others
dating from the old régime are yet well preserved
and are in daily use as chapels. From belfries in
Florida, Texas, New Mexico, Arizona, and California still sound bells that were cast in Old Spain.
At New Orleans the Cabildo, though standing in
the French Quarter, was built in Spanish days.
Likewise the old cathedral there is a heritage from
Spain and not from France. These Spanish survivals from the olden time have furnished the motif
for a new type of architecture in Florida and the

Southwest that has become one of the most distinctive American possessions. In Florida, Texas, Arizona, and California the type is dominated by mission architecture. In New Mexico it is strongly modified by that native culture which found expression in pueblo building.

There are still other marks of Spanish days on our southern border. We see them in social, religious, economic, and even in legal practices. Everywhere in the Southwest there are quaint church customs brought from Spain or Mexico by the early pioneers. At Christmas time in San Antonio one can see Las Posadas enacted. California has her Portolá festival, her rodeos, and her Mission Play. From the Spaniard the American cowboy inherited his trade, his horse, his outfit, his lingo, and his methods. Spain is stamped on our land surveys. From Sacramento to St. Augustine nearly everybody holds his acres by a title going back to Mexico or Madrid. Most of the farms, in a wide swath along the border, are divisions of famous grants which are still known by their original Spanish names. In the realm of law, principles regarding mines, water rights on streams, and the property rights of women—to mention only a few —have been retained from the Spanish régime. From our Spanish forerunners in the Southwest we got our first lesson in irrigation, that art which has become one of our primary southwestern interests.

Among the most priceless treasures of any country are its historical records and its folklore. And what a heritage in this realm was left us by the old Spanish days! Wagner collected a hundred and seventy-seven works dealing with the borderlands and printed before the end of the eighteenth century. And this does not take into account the still unpublished treasures with which the archives of Spain and Mexico abound. These monuments of the past include narratives of heroic adventure, like the expeditions of Cabeza de Vaca, De Soto, Friar Marcos, Coronado, Espejo, and Oñate; the actual diaries of the epic journeys of dauntless men, like De León, Terán, Vizcaíno, Garcés, Anza, Escalante, De Mézières, Portolá, Serra, Crespi, and Palóu. There is Villagrá's precious metrical history of the founding of New Mexico, a thrilling tale of human exploit in a desert land. There are histories of these border provinces by Padilla, Benavides, Vetancourt, Espinosa, Arricivita, Morfi, Venegas, Kino, Ortega, and Palóu. These carefully written and beautifully printed old chronicles in many instances still stand as the authoritative word on the regions with which they deal. We Anglo-Ameri-

[101]

cans, with our professed advancement in historical science, have never even caught up with them, and probably never shall.

Not the least important part of our heritage has been the Hispanic appeal to the imagination. The Spanish occupation has furnished theme and color for myriad writers, great and small. Lomax and Dobie, Lummis and Willa Cather, Bret Harte and Espinosa have shown that these inter-American bounds have a Spain-tinged folklore as rich as that of the Scottish border embalmed by Sir Walter Scott.

Lastly, these borderlands provide the historical background to our relations with Spain and Spanish America today. Born in international exigencies, and nurtured in race contacts, these fringes have always had vast international significance. International understanding is more than half a matter of tradition and psychology, and our national repute in Latin America and Spain even now is to a very large extent a reflection of history. Correctly or incorrectly, our neighbors remember this borderland tale.

Half of our national territory was once a part of the Spanish Empire—only the fringes, it is true, but legally a part of it, just the same. The English shouldered the Spaniards out of Georgia and Florida. Napoleon, in violation of a solemn promise not to alienate it, sold to the United States the vast area called Louisiana, embracing two-thirds of the Mississippi Valley, and only tardily, grudgingly and by force of necessity did Spain acknowledge our title.

The United States took advantage of Spain's trouble with her colonies to round out her border on the Gulf of Mexico. Yielding once more to necessity, Spain ceded to the United States all her claims to Oregon and British Columbia, as a means of retaining Texas.

Americans settled in Texas with the full consent of Mexico, and by a perfectly legal process. Friction resulted, the Americans arose in revolt, set up a republic, and extended its boundary to the Rio Grande. It matters little to Mexican psychology, unless Mexicans are rightly informed, that the Americans had grievances. In the face of Mexican opposition Texas was annexed. The United States tried to purchase California, but Mexico refused to sell. Then purchase was made unnecessary—the soldier accomplished what settler and diplomat had left undone. The annexation of Texas eventuated in war; the price of war to Mexico was more than half her national patrimony. Then came the Gadsden Purchase, cutting off another slice, a bargain for which Mexicans still execrate Santa Anna. Finally, in 1898, the United States by means of war shook the last of the colonies from the Spanish tree, and part of them,—Puerto Rico and the Philippines—fell into our basket.

I am not pretending here to assess or even to suggest the measure of merit or blame on either side in any instance. Wherever the balance may be, it is not surprising that Mexico remembers these border episodes. Through them all South America looked on, sympathizing with Mexico in her losses and wondering how far the process would go. Other factors enter in, but in trying to understand Latin American attitude toward us, we cannot overlook the influence of the old Spanish Borderlands, as the zone of contact, the scene of a long series of conflicts, ending in territorial transfers.

Fortunately there is another side to the shield. For a drop of gall there are two drops of cordial. If these borderlands have left some unpleasant memories between two peoples, they are partly offset by the bonds of a common inheritance. The historical ties between the borderlands and Spanish America are strong and closely drawn. Our oldest traditions run back to Spain and Mexico. Our earliest heroes are also Mexico's heroes. We teach our children many of the same hero tales that they teach their children. In the beginning Florida, New Mexico, Texas, Arizona, and California were but projections of New Spain northward. Our explorers came chiefly from a Mexican base. As Spanish heroes they went to the "far north." As our heroes they came from the "far south." But their names—De Soto, Coronado, Cabrillo, De León, Oñate, Anza, Garcés, and Escalante—are the same in either case; in the books read by their children and in the books read by our children.

Our great missionary heroes are their missionary heroes—Reynoso, Benavides, Ramírez, Casañas, Massanet, Margil, Serra, and Crespi. A year ago the State of California chose two names to represent it in the hall of fame at the capitol in Washington. One name was chosen unanimously and without dissent. That one was Father Junípero Serra. He is California's acknowledged hero. He is also Spain's hero and Mexico's hero. Two decades before he came to us he came to Mexico. His first American home was the celebrated College of San Fernando. Nine years he pursued his apostolic labors in the Sierra Gorda north of Querétaro. Once he was assigned to the Apache missions in Texas, but Fate directed his course to the farther West, and instead he went to California. Serra is a link binding Spain, Mexico, and California. In Mallorca a monument commemorates him as a Spanish hero. In Washington a statue will commemorate him as a California hero. Some day there will be a statue of him in

Mexico. Then these three monuments will symbolize the common heritage of Spain, Mexico, and California. And other states have other heroes, binding them likewise to Mexico and Spain.

It is we in the borderlands who have the strongest historical bonds with our Latin neighbors. We of all North Americans best know and appreciate their brilliant minds, their generous hearts, and their delicate culture. We of all North Americans most prize the unmistakable Spanish touch which our fore-runners gave our once Spanish lands. It would be only fitting if we of the borderlands should be foremost in a fair-minded appraisal of our common historical heritage, foremost in the study of our common problems, and foremost in making closer and stronger the bonds of true international understanding.

[1] This does not include the vastly larger native population.

[2] Not alone Spanish fancy ran astray here. Laudonnière, the Frenchman, went Ponce de León one better, for one of his scouts actually saw and conversed with men who had drunk at the Fountain of Youth, and had already comfortably passed their two hundred and fiftieth birthdays.

THE MISSION AS A FRONTIER IN-
STITUTION IN THE SPANISH-
AMERICAN COLONIES *

I

OF the missions in Spanish America much has been
written. But most of what has been produced con-
sists of chronicles of the deeds of the Fathers, po-
lemic discussions by sectarian partisans, or senti-
mental effusions with literary, edifying, or financial
intent. They deal with the heroic exploits of indi-
viduals, with mooted questions of belief and practice, or with the romance that hovers around the
mission ruins. All this is very well, and not to be
ridiculed, but it is none the less true that little has
been said of these missions in their relation to the
general Spanish colonial system, of which they were
an integral and a most important part.

One of the marvels in the history of the modern
world is the way in which that little Iberian nation,
Spain, when most of her blood and treasure were
absorbed in European wars, with a handful of men

* Faculty Research Lecture, University of California, Berkeley, March, 1917. Printed in the American Historical Review,
Vol. XXIII, No. 1, Oct., 1917.

took possession of the Caribbean archipelago, and by rapid yet steady advance spread her culture, her religion, her law, and her language over more than half of the two American continents, where they still are dominant and still are secure—in South America, Central America, and a large fraction of North America, for more than fifty million people in America today are tinged with Spanish blood, still speak the Spanish language, still worship at the altar set up by the Catholic kings, still live under laws essentially Spanish, and still possess a culture inherited from Spain.

These results are an index of the vigor and the virility of Spain's frontier forces; they should give pause to those who glibly speak of Spain's failure as a colonizing nation; and they suggest the importance of a thoughtful study of Spain's frontier institutions and methods. Professor Turner has devoted his life to a study of the Anglo-American frontier, and rich has been his reward. Scarcely less conspicuous in the history of the Western world than the advance of the Anglo-American frontier has been the spread of Spanish culture, and for him who interprets, with Turner's insight, the methods and the significance of the Spanish-American frontier, there awaits a recognition not less marked or less deserved.

Whoever essays this task, whoever undertakes to

interpret the means by which Spain extended her rule, her language, her law, and her traditions, over the frontiers of her vast American possessions, must give close attention to the Indian missions, for in that work they constituted a primary agency. Each of the colonizing nations in America had its peculiar frontier institutions and classes. In the French colonies the pioneers of pioneers were the fur-trader and the missionary. Penetrating the innermost wilds of the continent, one in search of the beaver, the other in quest of souls to save, together they extended the French domains, and brought the savage tribes into friendly relations with the French government, and into profitable relations with the Gallic outposts. In the English colonies the fur-trader blazed the way and opened new trails, but it was the backwoods settler who hewed down the forest, and step by step drove back the Indian. In the Spanish colonies the men to whom fell the task of extending and holding the frontiers were the conquistador, the presidial soldier, the miner, the cattleman, and the missionary.

All of these factors were important; but in a study of frontier institutions in general, and in an endeavor in particular to understand the methods and forces by which Spain's frontiers were extended, held, and developed, one is more and more impressed with the importance of the mission as a

[109]

pioneering agency. Taking for granted for the moment its very obvious religious aspects, I shall here devote my attention more especially to the mission's political and social meaning. My point of view embraces all of New Spain—all of the Spanish colonies, indeed—but more particularly the northern provinces, from Sinaloa to Texas, from Florida to California. My conclusions are based on a study of documents, unprinted for the most part, which have been gathered mainly from the archives of Mexico and Spain.

II

The function of the mission, viewed from the political standpoint, will be better understood if it is considered in its historical relations. The central interest around which the mission was built was the Indian. In respect to the native, the Spanish sovereigns from the outset had three fundamental purposes. They desired to convert him, to civilize him, and to utilize him. To serve these three purposes there was devised, out of the experience of the early conquerors, the *encomienda* system. It was soon found that if the savage were to be converted, or disciplined, or utilized, he must be put under control. To provide such control, the natives were distributed among Spaniards, who held them in trust, or in *encomienda*. The trustee, or *encomendero,* as he was called, was strictly charged by the sovereign, as a condition of his grant, to provide for the protection, the conversion, and the civilization of the aborigines. In return he was empowered to utilize their labor, sharing the profits with the king. To provide spiritual instruction and to conduct schools for the natives—for Indian schools were prescribed and maintained—the *encomenderos* were required to support the necessary clerics, by whom the instruction was given.

But the native had his own notions, especially about being exploited, and he sometimes fled to the woods. It was soon discovered, therefore, that in order properly to convert, instruct and employ the Indian, he must be kept in a fixed place of residence. This need was early reported to the sovereigns by *encomenderos* and religious alike, and it soon became a law that Indians must be congregated in pueblos, by force if necessary, and made to stay there. The pueblos were modelled on the Spanish towns, and were designed not alone as a means of control, but as schools in self-control as well.

Thus, during the early years of the conquest, the natives were largely in the hands of the *encomenderos,* mainly secular landholders and mining men. The friars, and afterward the Jesuit priests, came in great numbers, to preach and teach, but at first they lacked the authority of later days. In 1574 there were in the conquered districts of Spanish America nearly nine thousand Indian towns, containing about one and a half million adult males, representing some five million people, subject to tribute. These nine thousand towns were *encomiendas* of the king and some four thousand other *encomenderos*.

The *encomienda* system then, by intention, was benevolent. It was designed for the conversion and the civilization of the native, as well as for the exploitation of his labor. But the flesh is weak, and the system was abused. The obligations to protect, convert, and civilize were too often forgotten, and the right to utilize was frequently perverted into license. Practical slavery soon resulted, and the *encomienda* system became the black spot in the Spanish-American code. Philanthropists, led by Las Casas, begged for reform; abuses were checked, and *encomiendas* were gradually, though slowly, abolished.

This improvement was made easier by the decreasing attractiveness of *encomiendas* as the conquest proceeded to the outlying districts. The sedentary Indians of central Mexico and of Peru had been fairly docile, had possessed a steady food supply and fixed homes, were accustomed to labor, and

were worth exploiting. The wilder tribes encountered later—the Chichimecos, as they were called—
were hostile, had few crops, were unused to labor,
had no fixed villages, would not stand still to be
exploited, and so were hardly worth the candle.
Colonists were no longer so eager for *encomiendas*
as formerly, and were willing to escape the obliga-
tion to protect and civilize the wild tribes, which,
sometimes, were as uncomfortable burdens as cub-
tigers in a sack. Moreover, the sovereigns, with increasing emphasis, forbade the old-time abuses of
exploitation, but as strongly as before adhered to
the ideal of conversion and civilization. Here, then,
was a wider opening for the missionary, and to him
was entrusted, or upon him was thrust, not only the
old work of conversion, but a broader element of
responsibility and control. On the northern frontier,
therefore, especially among the roving tribes, the
place of the discredited *encomendero* was largely
taken by the missionary, and that of the *encomienda*
by the mission, the design being to check the evils of
exploitation, and at the same time to realize the
ideal of conversion, protection, and civilization.

These missionaries became a veritable corps of
Indian agents, serving both Church and State. The
double capacity in which they functioned was made
easy and natural by the close union between Church

and State in Spanish America, where the king exercised the real patronato, and where the viceroys were sometimes archbishops as well.

Under these conditions, in the seventeenth and eighteenth centuries, on the expanding frontiers of Spanish America, missions became well-nigh universal. In South America the outstanding examples of success were the Jesuit missions in Paraguay. Conspicuous in North America were the great Franciscan establishments in Alta California, the last of Spain's major conquests. Not here alone, however, but everywhere on the northern frontier missions played their part—in Sinaloa, Sonora, and California; in Chihuahua, Coahuila, Nuevo León, and Nuevo Santander; in Florida, New Mexico, Texas, and Arizona. If there were twenty-one missions in Alta California, there were as many in Texas, more in Florida, and twice as many in New Mexico. At one time the California missions had over thirty thousand Indians under instruction; a century and a half earlier the missions of Florida and New Mexico had perhaps an equal number.

The missionary work on the outer frontier of New Spain was conducted chiefly by Franciscans, Jesuits, and Dominicans. The northeastern field fell mainly to the Franciscans, who entered Coahuila, Nuevo León, Nuevo Santander, New Mexico, Texas, and Florida. To the northwest came the

Jesuits, who, after withdrawing from Florida, worked especially in Sinaloa, Sonora, Chihuahua, Lower California, and Arizona. In 1767 the Jesuits were expelled from all Spanish America, and their places taken by the other orders. To Lower California then came the Dominicans, to Sonora and Arizona the Franciscans of the College of the Holy Cross of Querétaro, and to Alta California the Franciscans of the College of San Fernando, in the City of Mexico.

III

The missions, then, like the presidios, or garrisons, were characteristically and designedly frontier institutions, and it is as pioneer agencies that they must be studied. This is true whether they be considered from the religious, the political, or the social standpoint. As religious institutions they were designed to introduce the Faith among the heathen. Having done this, their function was to cease. Being designed for the frontier, they were intended to be temporary. As soon as his work was finished at one outpost, the missionary was expected to move on to another. In the theory of the law, within ten years each mission must be turned over to the parish clergy, and the common mission lands distributed among the Indians. But this law had

[115]

been based on experience with the more advanced tribes of Mexico, Central America, and Perú. On the northern frontier, among the barbarian tribes, a longer period of tutelage was always found necessary.

The result, almost without fail, was a struggle over secularization. So long as the Indians were under the missionaries, their lands were secure from the land-grabber. The land-grabber always, therefore, urged the fulfillment of the ten-year law, just as the "squatter," the "sooner," and the "boomer" have always urged the opening of our Indian reservations to white settlers. But the missionaries always knew the danger and they always resisted secularization until their work was finished. Sooner, or later, however, with the disappearance of frontier conditions, the missionary was expected to move on. His religious task was beside the soldier, *entre infieles,* in the outposts of civilization.

But the missionaries were not alone religious agents. Designedly in part and incidentally in part, they were political and civilizing agents of a very positive sort, and as such they constituted a vital feature of Spain's pioneering system. From the standpoint of the Church, and as viewed by themselves, their principal work, first, last, and always, was to spread the Faith. To doubt this is to confess complete and disqualifying ignorance of the great

[116]

mass of existing missionary correspondence printed
and unprinted, so fraught with unmistakable proofs
of the religious zeal and devotion of the vast majority of the missionaries. It is quite true, as Engelhardt says, that they "came not as scientists, as
geographers, as school-masters, nor as philanthropists, eager to uplift the people in a worldly sense,
to the exclusion or neglect of the religious duties
pointed out by Christ." But it is equally true, and
greatly to their credit, that incidentally from their
own standpoint and designedly from that of the
government, they were all these and more, and that
to all these and other services they frequently and
justly made claim when they asked for government
aid.

The missions, then, were agencies of the State as
well as of the Church. They served not alone to
Christianize the frontier, but also to aid in extending, holding, and civilizing it. Since Christianity
was the basic element of European civilization and
since it was the acknowledged duty of the State to
extend the Faith, the first task of the missionary,
from the standpoint of both State and Church, was
to convert the heathen. But neither the State nor the
Church—nor the missionary himself—considered
the work of the mission as ending here. If the Indian
were to become either a worthy Christian or a desirable subject he must be disciplined in the rudi-

[117]

ments of civilized life. The task of giving the discipline was likewise turned over to the missionary. Hence, the missions were designed to be not only Christian seminaries, but in addition were outposts for the control and training schools for the civilizing of the frontier.

Since they served the State, the missions were financed by the State. It is a patent fact, and scarcely needs demonstrating, that they were maintained to a very considerable extent by the royal treasury. The Franciscan missions of New Spain in the eighteenth century had four principal means of support. The annual stipends of the missionaries (the *sinodos*) were usually paid by the government. These *sinodos* varied in amount according to the remoteness of the missions, and on the northernmost frontier were usually $450 for each missionary. In 1758, for example, a report on the Franciscan missions shows that the treasury of New Spain was annually paying *sinodos* for twelve Querétaro friars in Coahuila and Texas, six Jaliscans in Coahuila, eleven Zacatecans in Texas, ten Fernandinos in the Sierra Gorda, six Jaliscans in Nayarit, twenty-two Zacatecans in Nuevo León and Nueva Vizcaya, seventeen Zacatecans in Nuevo Santander, five San Diegans in the Sierra Gorda, and thirty-four friars of the Provincia del Santo Evangelio in New Mexico, or, in all, 123 friars, at an average of about 350 pesos

each. This report did not include the Franciscans of
the Provincia de Campeche or the Yslas de Barlovento, for which separate reports had been asked.
Other appropriations were made for Franciscan
missionaries in the Marianas and the Philippine Islands, dependencies of New Spain. And this report
does not include royal funds devoted to the support
of the Jesuits and other missionary laborers in the
viceroyalty.

Besides the *sínodos,* the government regularly
furnished the missionaries with military protection,
detaching from the near-by presidios from two to
half a dozen or more soldiers for each mission. In
addition, the royal treasury usually made an initial
grant (*ayuda de costa*) of $1,000 to each mission,
to pay for bells, vestments, tools, and other expenses
of the founding, and in cases of emergency it frequently made special grants for building or other
purposes.

These government subsidies did not preclude
gifts, or alms, which were constantly sought and
often obtained. In the founding of new missions the
older establishments were expected to give aid, and
if able they did respond in liberal measure. And
then there were private endowments. Classic examples of such contributions on the northern frontier were the gifts of Don Pedro de Terreros, later
Conde de Regla, who offered $150,000 to found

Apache missions in Coahuila and Texas, and the Jesuit Fondo Piadoso of California. This latter Pious Fund, begun in 1697, grew by a variety of gifts to such an amount that the missions of Lower California were largely supported by the income. On the expulsion of the Jesuits in 1767 the fund was taken over by the government, and became the principal means of support of the new Franciscan missions of Alta California, besides being devoted in part to secular purposes. Even in Alta California, however, the royal treasury paid the wages (*sueldos*) of the mission guards, and gave other financial aid.

Finally, the Indians of the missions were expected soon to become self-supporting, and, indeed, in many cases they did acquire large wealth through stock-raising and agricultural pursuits. But not a penny of this belonged to the missionaries, and the annual *sínodos,* or salaries, continued to be paid from other sources, from the Pious Fund in California, and from the royal treasury generally elsewhere.

While it is thus true that the missions were supported to a very considerable degree by the royal treasury, it is just as plain that the amount of government aid, and the ease with which it was obtained, depended largely upon the extent to which political ends could be combined with religious purposes. The importance of political necessity in loosening the royal purse-strings is seen at every turn in the history of Spanish North America. Knowing the strength of a political appeal, the missionaries generally made use of it in their requests for aid. While the monarchs ever used pious phrases, and praised the work of the padres—without hypocrisy no doubt—the royal pocket-book was more readily opened to found new missions if there was a political as well as a religious object to be gained.

Typical examples of this fact are seen in the histories of Texas and California. The missionaries of the northern frontier had long had their eyes on the "Kingdom of the Texas" as a promising field of labor, and had appealed to the government for aid in cultivating it. But in vain, till La Salle planted a French colony at Matagorda Bay. Then the royal pocket-book was opened, and funds were provided for missions in eastern Texas. The French danger passed for the moment and the missions were withdrawn. Then for another decade Father Hidalgo begged without success for funds and authority to re-establish the missions. But when St. Denis, agent of the French governor of Louisiana, intruded himself into Coahuila, the Spanish government at once gave liberal support for the refounding of the missions, to aid in restraining the threatening French.

The case was the same for California. Since the time of Vizcaíno the missionaries had clamored for funds and permission to found missions at San Diego and Monterey. In 1620 Father Ascensión, who had been with Vizcaíno eighteen years before, wrote, "I do not know what security His Majesty can have in his conscience for delaying so long to send ministers of the Gospel to this realm of California," and, during the next century and a half, a hundred others echoed this admonition. But all to no purpose till the Russian Bear began to amble or to threaten to amble down the Pacific Coast. Then money was forthcoming, and then missionaries were sent to help hold the country for the crown. On this point Father Engelhardt correctly remarks:

The missionaries, who generally offered to undergo any hardships in order to convert the Indians, appear to have been enlisted merely for the purpose of securing the territory for the Spanish king . . . [and] the Spanish government would not have sent ships and troops to the northwest if the Russians had not crept down the Pacific coast. . . .

He continues:

The men who presumed to guide the destinies of Spain then, and, as a rule ever since, cared not for the success of Religion or the welfare of its ministers except in so far as both could be used to promote political schemes.

In this last assertion, I think, Father Engelhardt is too hard on the Spanish monarchs. Their pious phrases were not mere hypocrisy. They were truly desirous of spreading the Faith. But they were terribly hard up, and they had little means to support religious projects unless they contributed to both political and religious ends.

IV

The value of the missionaries as frontier agents was thus clearly recognized, and their services were thus consciously utilized by the government. In the first place, the missionaries were often the most useful of explorers and diplomatic agents. The unattended missionary could sometimes go unmolested, and without arousing suspicion and hostility, into districts where the soldier was not welcome, while by their training they were the persons best fitted to record what they saw and to report what should be done. So they were often sent alone to explore new frontiers, as peace emissaries to hostile tribes, or as chroniclers of expeditions led by others. Hence it is that the best of the diaries of early exploration in the Southwest—and, indeed, in most of Spanish America—were written by the missionaries.

As illustrations of this kind of frontier service on the part of the missionaries we have but to recall the example of Friar Marcos, who was sent by Viceroy Mendoza to seek the Seven Cities in New Mexico; the rediscovery of that province, under the viceroy's patronage, by the party led by Fray Agustín Rodríguez; the expeditions of Father Larios, unattended, into Coahuila; the forty or more journeys of Father Kino across the deserts of Sonora, and his demonstration that California was a peninsula, not an island, as most men had thought; the part played by Kino in pacifying the revolt of the Pimas in 1695, and in making the frontier safe for settlers; the diplomatic errands of Fathers Calahorra and Ramírez, sent by the governors of Texas to the hostile northern tribes; the lone travels of Father Garcés, of two thousand miles or more, over untrod trails, in Arizona, California, and New Mexico, seeking a better route to California; and the expedition of Fathers Domínguez and Escalante, pathfinders for an equal distance in and about the Great Basin between the Rockies and the California Sierras.

The missions served also as a means of defense

of the king's dominions. This explains why the
government was more willing to support missions
when the frontier needed protection than at other
times, as in the cases, already cited, of Texas and
California. It is significant, too, in this connection,
that the Real Hacienda, or royal fisc, charged the
expenses for presidios and missions both to the
same account, the Ramo de Guerra, or War De-
partment. In a report for New Spain made in 1758
a treasury official casually remarked, "Presidios are
erected and missions founded in *tierra firme* when-
ever it is necessary to defend conquered districts
from the hostilities and invasions of warlike, barbarian tribes, and to plant and extend our Holy
Faith, for which purposes *juntas de guerra y hacienda* are held." It is indeed true that appropriations
for missions were frequently made and that permission to found missions was often given in councils of
war and finance.

Reasons for this practice are not far to seek. The
missionaries counteracted foreign influence among
their neophytes, deterred them from molesting the
interior settlements, and secured their aid in holding back more distant tribes. Nearly every army
that was led from San Antonio, Texas, in the eighteenth century, against hostile Apaches and Coman-
ches, contained a strong contingent of mission Indians, who fought side by side with the Spaniards.

Father Kino was relied upon by the military leaders of Sonora to obtain the aid of the Pimas, his beloved neophytes, in defense of the Sonora settlements. When he was assigned to California, in company with Salvatierra, the authorities of Sonora protested, on the ground that, through his influence over the natives, he was a better means of protection to the province than a whole company of soldiers. When a Spanish expedition was organized to attack the Apaches, Kino was sent ahead to arouse and enlist the Pima allies. When the Pimas put the Apaches to flight, it was Kino to whom they sent the count of the enemy's dead, recorded by notches on a pole; on the same occasion it was Kino who received the thanks of citizens and officials of the province; and, when doubt was expressed as to what the Pimas had accomplished, it was Kino who rode a hundred miles or more to count the scalps of the vanquished foe, as evidence with which to vindicate his Pima friends.

The very mission plants were constructed and often served as fortresses, not alone for padres and neophytes, but for near-by settlers, too. A typical well-built mission was ranged round a great court or patio, protected on all sides by the buildings, whose walls were sometimes eight feet thick. In hostile countries these buildings were often enclosed within massive protecting walls. In 1740

President Santa Ana wrote that Mission Valero, at San Antonio, Texas, was better able to withstand a siege than any of the three presidios of the province. Twenty-two years later the same mission was surrounded by a wall, and over the gate was a tower, equipped with muskets, ammunition, and three cannon. At the same time the mission of San José, near by, was called "a castle" which more than once had been proof against the Apaches.

Not only were the missionaries consciously utilized as political agents to hold the frontier, but they often served, on their own motion or with the co-operation of the secular authority, as "promoters" of the unoccupied districts. They sent home reports of the outlying tribes, of the advantages of obtaining their friendship, of the danger of foreign intrusions, of the wealth and attractions of the country, and of the opportunities to extend the king's dominion. Frequently, indeed, they were called to Mexico, or even to Spain, to sit in the royal councils, where their expert opinions often furnished the primary basis of a decision to occupy a new outpost. For examples of this service, near at home, we have but to recall Escobar, Benavides, and Ayeta of New Mexico, Massanet, Hidalgo, and Santa Ana of Texas, Kino of Lower California, and Serra of Alta California. Other parts of America furnished many similar examples. Thus consciously or un-

[127]

consciously, directly or indirectly, with or without secular initiative, the missionaries served as most active promoters, one might even call them "boosters," of the frontier.

V

But the missionaries helped not only to extend and hold and promote the frontier; more significantly still, they helped to civilize it. And this is the kernel of my theme. Spain possessed high ideals, but she had peculiar difficulties with which to contend. She laid claim to the lion's share of the two Americas, but her population was small and little of it could be spared to people the New World. On the other hand, her colonial policy, excelled in humanitarian principles by that of no other country, looked to the preservation of the natives and to their absorption into the body politic. Lacking Spaniards to colonize the frontier, she would colonize it with the aborigines. Such a plan called not only for the subjugation and control of the natives, but for their civilization as well. To accomplish this end the rulers of Spain again utilized the religious and humanitarian zeal of the missionaries, choosing them to be to the Indians not only preachers, but also teachers and disciplinarians as well. To the extent that this work succeeded it became possible

[128]

to people the frontier with civilized natives, and thus to supply the lack of European colonists. This desire was quite in harmony with the religious aims of the missionaries, who found temporal discipline indispensable to the best work of Christianization.

Hence it is that in the Spanish system—as distinguished from the French, for example—the essence of the mission was the discipline, religious, moral, social, and industrial, which it afforded. The very physical arrangement of the mission was determined with a view to discipline. The central feature of every successful mission was the Indian village, or pueblo. The settled tribes, such as the Pueblo Indians of New Mexico, or the Pimas of Arizona, could be instructed in their native towns, but wandering and scattered tribes must be assembled and established in pueblos, and kept there, by force if necessary. The reason why the missions of eastern Texas failed was that the Indians refused to settle in pueblos, and without more soldiers than were available it was impossible to control them. It was on this question that Father Serra split with Governor Neve regarding the Santa Barbara Indians in California. To save expense for soldiers, Neve urged that the friars should minister to the Indians in their native *rancherías*. But the missionaries protested that by this arrangement the Indians could not be disciplined. The plan was given up, therefore, and instead the Indians were congregated in great towns at San Buenaventura and Santa Barbara. Thus, the pueblo was essential to the functioning of the mission, as it had been to the *encomienda.*

Discipline called for control, and this was placed largely in the hands of the missionaries. The Franciscan rule was two friars for each mission, but in many instances there was only one. The need of more was often urged. For lack of man power the Jesuit missionaries of western Mexico usually worked singly.

As a symbol of force, and to afford protection for missionaries and mission Indians, as well as to hold the frontier against savages and foreigners, presidios, or garrisons, were established near by. And thus, across the continent, from San Agustín to San Francisco, stretched a long and slender line of presidios—San Agustín, Apalache, Pensacola, Los Adaes, La Bahía, San Antonio, San Juan Bautista, Rio Grande, San Sabá, El Paso, Santa Fé, Janos, Fronteras, Terrenate, Tubac, Altár, San Diego, Santa Barbara, Monterey, and San Francisco—a line more than twice as long as the Rhine-Danube frontier held by the Romans, from whom Spain learned her lesson in frontier defense.

To assist the missionaries in their work of disciplining and instructing the neophytes, each mission was usually provided with two or more soldiers from the nearest presidio. To help in recovering runaways—for the Indians frequently did abscond —special detachments of soldiers were furnished. The impression is often given that the missionaries objected to the presence of soldiers at the missions, but as a rule the case was quite the contrary. What they did object to were unsuitable soldiers, and outside interference in the selection and control of the guard. It is true, indeed, that immoral or insubordinate soldiers were deemed a nuisance, and that since the presidials were largely half-breeds—mestizos or mulattoes—and often jailbirds at that, this type was all too common. But in general, military aid was demanded, and complaint of its inadequacy was constantly made. On this point the testimony of Fray Romualdo Cartagena, guardian of the College of Santa Cruz de Querétaro, is valid. In a report made in 1772, still in manuscript, he wrote:

What gives these missions their permanency is the aid which they receive from the Catholic arms. Without them pueblos are frequently abandoned, and ministers are murdered by the barbarians. It is seen every day that in missions where there are no soldiers there is no success, for the Indians, being children of fear, are more strongly appealed to by the glistening of the sword than by the voice of five missionaries. Soldiers are necessary to defend the Indians from the enemy, and to keep an eye on the mission Indians, now to encourage them, now to carry news to the nearest presidio in case of trouble. For the spiritual and temporal progress of the missions two soldiers are needed, for the Indians cannot be trusted, especially in new conversions.

This is the testimony of missionaries themselves. That protection was indeed necessary is shown by the martyrdom of missionaries on nearly every frontier—of Father Segura and his entire band of Jesuits in Virginia in 1571; of Father Saeta in Sonora; of Fathers Ganzábal, Silva, Terreros, and Santiesteban in Texas; of a score of Jesuits in western Mexico; of other scores in South America; of Fathers Carranco and Tamaral in Lower California; of Father Luis Jayme at San Diego (Alta California); of Father Garcés and his three companions at Yuma, on the Colorado River; and of the twenty-one Franciscans in the single uprising in New Mexico in 1680. But these martyrdoms were only occasional, and the principal business of the soldiers was to assist the missionaries in the routine of disciplining and civilizing the neophytes.

As teachers, and as an example to new converts, it was the custom to place in each new mission a few Indian families from the older missions. After a time they might return to their former homes. As Father Romualdo remarked: "It is all the better if these families be related to the new, for this insures the permanence of the latter in the missions, while if they do flee it is easier to recover them by means of their relatives than through strangers." And a common language was of course an important asset.

Notable among the Indians utilized as teachers and colonists in the northern missions were the Tlascaltecans, of Tlascala, the native city of Mexico made famous by Prescott. Having been subdued by Cortés, the Tlascaltecans became the most trusted supporters of the Spaniards, as they had been the most obstinate foes of the "Triple Alliance," and, after playing an important part in the conquest of the Valley of Mexico they became a regular factor in the extension of Spanish rule over the north country. Thus, when San Luis Potosí had been conquered, colonies of Tlascaltecans were sent to teach the more barbarous natives of that district both loyalty to the Spaniards and the rudiments of civilization. In Saltillo a large colony of Tlascaltecans was established by Urdiñola at the end of the sixteenth century, and became the mother colony from which numerous off-shoots were planted at the new missions and villages further north. At one time a hundred families of Tlascaltecans were ordered sent to Pensacola; in 1755 they figured in the plans for a missionary colony on Trinity River, in Texas; two years later a little band of them were sent to the San Sabá mission in western Texas to assist in civilizing the Apaches; and twenty years afterward it was proposed that a settlement, with Tlascalans as a nucleus, be established far to the north, on the upper Red River, among the Wichita Indians of Texas and Oklahoma. To help in civilizing the mission Indians of Jalisco, Sinaloa, and Sonora, the Tarascans of Michoacán were utilized; further north, the Opatas, of southern Sonora, were sent into Arizona as teachers of the Pimas; to help him tame the natives of Alta California, Serra brought Christianized Indians from the Peninsula.

VI

Discipline and the elements of European civilization were imparted at the missions through religious instruction, through industrial training, and, among more advanced natives, by means of rudimentary teaching in arts and letters.

Every mission was in the first place a Christian seminary, designed to give religious discipline. Religious instruction, of the elementary sort suited to the occasion, was imparted by a definite routine, based on long experience, and administered with much practical sense and regard for local conditions. Aside from the fundamental cultural concepts involved in Christianity, this religious instruction in itself involved a most important means of assimilation. By the laws of the Indies the missionaries were enjoined to instruct the neophytes in their native tongues, and in the colleges and seminaries professorships were established to teach them. But it was found that, just as the natives lacked the concepts, the Indian languages lacked the terms in which properly to convey the meaning of the Christian doctrine. Moreover, on some frontiers there were so many dialects that it was impossible for the friars to learn them. This was pre-eminently true of the lower Rio Grande region, where, we are told, there were over two hundred dialects, more than twenty of which were quite distinct. On this point Father Ortiz wrote in 1745:

The ministers who have learned some language of the Indians of these missions assert that it is impossible to compose a catechism in their idiom, because of the lack of terms in which to explain matters of faith, and the best informed interpreters say the same. There are as many languages as there are tribes, which in these missions aggregate more than two hundred. . . . Although they mingle and understand each other to some extent, there are twenty languages used commonly by the greater number of the tribes. And since they are new to us, and there are no schools in which to learn them, and since the Fathers are occupied with ministering to the spiritual and temporal needs of the Indians, and in recovering those who flee, they can hardly be held blameworthy for not learning the native tongues.

[135]

For these reasons, on the northern frontier instruction was usually given in Spanish, through interpreters at first, and directly as soon as the Indians learned the language of the padres. In the case of children, who were the chief consideration, this was quickly done. And thus incidentally a long step toward assimilation was accomplished, for we all know the importance of language in the fusing of races and cultures. The firmness of the hold of the Spanish language upon any land touched by Spain, however lightly, has often been noted. In America it was partly, perhaps largely, due to this teaching of the native children at the missions.

The routine of religious discipline established by the Franciscans in the missions taken over from the Jesuits in Sonora in 1767 was typical of all Franciscan missions, and was not essentially different from that of the other orders. It was described by Father Reyes, later Bishop Reyes, as follows:

Every day at sunrise the bells call the Indians to Mass. An old Indian, commonly called *mador,* and two *fiscales,* go through the whole pueblo, requiring all children and unmarried persons to go to the church, to take part in the devotion and silence of the Mass. This over, they repeat in concert, in Spanish, with the minister, the prayers and the Creed. At sunset this exercise is repeated at the door of the church, and is concluded with saying the rosary and chanting the *Salve* or the

[136]

Alabado. The *mador* and the *fiscales* are charged, on Sundays and feast days, to take care to require all men, women, and children to be present at Mass, with their poor clothes clean, and all washed and combed.

The very act of going to church involved a lesson in the amenities of civilization. There was virtue then as now in putting on one's "Sunday clothes."

On these days [Father Reyes continues] Mass is chanted with harps, violins [all played by the natives], and a choir of from four to six [native] men and women. In Lent all have been required to go to Mass daily. . . .

On Palm Sunday, at the head missions (*cabeceras*), that feast is observed with an image and processions. After Easter, censuses are made to ascertain what ones have complied with the Church. In the first years it seemed impossible to us missionaries to vanquish the rudeness of the Indians, and the difficulties of making them confess, and of administering communion. But lately all the young men and some of the old have confessed. In the principal pueblos, where the missionaries reside, many attend the sacraments on feast days. On the Feast of Santa María the rosary is sung through the pueblo. On other occasions they are permitted to have balls, diversions, and innocent games. But because they have attempted to prohibit superstitious balls and the scalp dance, the missionaries have encountered strong opposition from the [secular] superiors of the

[137]

province, who desire to let the Indians continue these excesses.

They contributed, no doubt, to the war spirit, and thus to the defense of the province against the Apaches.

VII

If the mission was a Christian seminary, it was scarcely less an industrial training school. Father Engelhardt writes:

It must be remembered that the friars came to California as messengers of Christ. They were not farmers, mechanics, or stock breeders. Those who, perhaps, had been engaged in such pursuits, had abandoned them for the higher occupation of the priest of God, and they had no desire to be further entangled in worldly business. In California, however [and he might have added, quite generally] the messengers of the Gospel had to introduce, teach, and supervise those very arts, trades, and occupations, before they could expect to make any headway with the truths of salvation. . . . As an absolutely necessary means to win the souls of the savages, these unworldly men accepted the disagreeable task of conducting huge farms, teaching and supervising various mechanical trades, having an eye on the livestock and herders, and making ends meet generally.

The civilizing function of the typical frontier mission, where the missionaries had charge of the temporalities as well as the spiritualities, was evident from the very nature of the mission plant. The church was ever the centre of the establishment, and the particular object of the minister's pride and care, but it was by no means the larger part. Each fully developed mission was a great industrial school, of which the largest, as in California, sometimes managed more than 2,000 Indians. There were weaving rooms, blacksmith shop, tannery, wine-press, and warehouses; there were irrigating ditches, vegetable gardens, and grain fields; and on the ranges roamed thousands of horses, cattle, sheep, and goats. Training in the care of fields and stock not only made the neophytes self-supporting, but afforded the discipline necessary for the rudiments of civilized life. The women were taught to cook, sew, spin, and weave; the men to fell the forest, build houses and churches, run the forge, tan leather, make ditches, tend cattle, and shear sheep.

Even in New Mexico, where the missionaries as a rule were not in charge of the temporalities—that is, of the economic interests of the Indians—and where the Indians had a well-established native agriculture, the friars were charged with their instruction in the arts and crafts, as well as with their religious education. And when the custodian, Father Benavides—later Bishop of Goa—wrote in 1630, after three decades of effort by the friars in that province, he was able to report fourteen missions, serving fifty-odd pueblos, each with its school, where the Indians were taught not only to sing, play musical instruments, read, and write, but, as Benavides puts it, "all the trades and polite deportment," all imparted by "the great industry of the Religious who converted them."

In controlling, supervising, and teaching the Indians, the missionaries were assisted by the soldier guards, who served as *mayordomos* of the fields, of the cattle and horse herds, of the sheep and goat ranches, and of the shops. In the older missions, even among the most backward tribes, it sometimes became possible to dispense with this service, as at San Antonio, Texas, where, it was reported in 1772, the Indians, once naked savages who lived on cactus apples and cotton-tail rabbits, had become so skilled and trustworthy that "without the aid of the Spaniards they harvest, from irrigated fields, maize, beans, and cotton in plenty, and Castilian cane for sugar. There are cattle, sheep and goats in abundance," all being the product of the care and labor of the natives.

The results of this industrial training at the missions were to be seen in the imposing structures that were built, the fertile farms that were tilled, and the great stock ranches that were tended, by erstwhile barbarians, civilized under the patient discipline

[140]

of the missionaries, assisted by soldier guards and imported Indian teachers, not in our Southwest alone, but on nearly every frontier of Spanish and Portuguese America, from Patagonia to California.

The missionaries transplanted to the frontiers and made known to the natives almost every conceivable domestic plant and animal of Europe. By requiring the Indians to work three days a week at community tasks, the Jesuits in Pimería Alta—to give a particular illustration—established at most of the missions flourishing ranches of horses, cattle, sheep, and goats, and opened fields and gardens for the cultivation of a wide variety of food plants. Kino wrote in 1710 of the Jesuit missions of Sonora and Arizona:

There are already thrifty and abundant fields . . . of wheat, maize, frijoles, chickpeas, beans, lentils, bastard chickpeas (garbanzos), etc. There are orchards, and in them vineyards for wine for the Masses; and fields of sweet cane for syrup and panocha, and with the favor of Heaven, before long, for sugar. There are many Castilian fruit trees, such as figs, quinces, oranges, pomegranates, peaches, apricots, pears, apples, mulberries, etc., and all sorts of garden stuff, such as cabbage, lettuce, onions, garlic, anise, pepper, mustard, mint, etc.

Other temporal means [he continues] are the numerous ranches, which are already stocked with cattle, sheep, and goats, many droves of mares, horses, and pack animals, mules as well as horses, for transportation and commerce, and very fat sheep, producing much tallow, suet, and soap, which is already manufactured in abundance.

An illustration of some of the more moderate material results is to be had in the following description of the four missions administered by the Querétaro friars in Texas, based on an official report made in 1762.

Besides the church, each mission had its *convento,* or residence, including cells for the friars, porter's lodge, refectory, kitchen, offices, workshops, and granary, usually all under a common roof and ranged round a patio. At San Antonio de Valero—the Alamo—the *convento* was a two-story structure fifty *varas* square with two patios and with arched cloisters above and below. The others were similar.

An important part of each mission was the workshop, for here the neophytes not only helped to supply their economic needs, but got an important part of their training for civilized life. At each of these four missions the Indians manufactured *mantas, terlingas, sayales, rebozos, frezadas,* and other common fabrics of wool and cotton. At Mission San Antonio the workshop contained four looms, and two store-rooms stocked with cotton, wool, cards, spindles, etc. At Concepción and San Francisco there were three looms each.

The neophytes of each mission lived in an Indian village or pueblo, closely connected with the church and *convento*. Of the pueblos of the four Queré-taran missions we have the fullest description of the one at Mission San Antonio de Valero. It consisted of seven rows of houses built of stone, with arched porticoes, doors, and windows. There was a plaza through which ran a water-ditch, bordered by willows and fruit trees. Within the plaza there was a curbed well, to supply water in case of a siege by the enemy. The pueblo was surrounded by a wall, and over the gate was a tower, with embrasures, three cannon, muskets, and ammunition. The houses were furnished with high beds, chests, metates, pots, kettles, and other domestic utensils. The pueblo of San Antonio was typical of all.

Agricultural and stock-raising activities had increased since 1745. At the four missions in question there were now grazing 4,897 head of cattle, 12,000 sheep and goats, and about 1,600 horses, and each mission had from thirty-seven to fifty yokes of working oxen. Of the four establishments San Francisco raised the most stock, having 2,262 head of cattle and 4,000 sheep and goats. Each mission had its ranch, some distance away, where the stock was kept, with one or more stone houses, occupied by the families of the overseers; the necessary corrals, farming implements, and carts; and tools for carpentry, masonry, and blacksmithing. Each mission had well-tilled fields, fenced in, and watered by good irrigating ditches with stone dams. In these fields maize, chile, beans, and cotton were raised in abundance, and in the *huertas* a large variety of garden truck.

This picture of the Texas missions is interesting, but in magnitude the establishments described are not to be compared with those in Jesuit Paraguay or with those in Franciscan California, where, in 1834, on the eve of the destruction of the missions, 31,000 Indians at twenty-one missions herded 396,-000 cattle, 62,000 horses and 321,000 hogs, sheep, and goats, and harvested 123,000 bushels of grain, and where corresponding skill and industry were shown by the neophytes in orchard, garden, wine-press, loom, shop, and forge.

VIII

The laws of the Indies prescribed and the missions provided a school for self-government, elementary and limited, it is true, but germane and potential nevertheless. This was effected by orga-

[144]

nizing the Indians of the mission into a pueblo, with civil and military officers, modelled upon the Spanish administration. When the mission was founded the secular head of the district—governor, captain, or alcalde—as representative of the king, formally organized the pueblo, appointed the native officers, and gave title to the four-league grant of land. In constituting the native government, wisdom dictated that use should be made of the existing Indian organization, natives of prestige being given the important offices. Thereafter the civil officers were chosen by a form of native election, under the supervision of the missionary, and approved by the secular head of the jurisdiction.

The civil officers were usually a governor, captain, alcaldes, and alguacil, who by law constituted a cabildo, or council. The military officers were a captain or a lieutenant, and subalterns, and were appointed by the secular head of the province, or by a native captain-general subject to approval by the secular head. The military officers had their own insignia, and, to give them prestige, separate benches were placed in the churches for the governor, alcalde, and council. In Sonora there was a topil, whose duty was to care for the community houses—a sort of free hostelry, open to all travelers, which seems to have been of native rather than of

Spanish origin. The Indians had their own jail, and inflicted minor punishments, prescribed by the minister. Indian overseers kept the laborers at their work, and indeed, much of the task of controlling the Indians was effected through Indian officers themselves. Of course it was the directing force of the padres and the restraining force of the near-by presidio which furnished the ultimate pressure.

This pueblo government was established among the more advanced tribes everywhere, and it succeeded in varying degrees. It was often a cause for conflict of jurisdiction, and in Alta California, where the natives were of tribes little advanced, it was strongly opposed by the friars. It has been called a farce, but certainly it was not so intended. It was not self-government any more than is student government in a primary school. But it was a means of control, and was a step toward self-government. It is one of the things, moreover, which help to explain how one or two missionaries and three or four soldiers could make an orderly town out of two or three thousand barbarians recently assembled from divers and sometimes mutually hostile tribes. So deeply was it impressed upon the Indians of New Mexico that some of them yet maintain their Spanish pueblo organization, and by it still govern themselves. And, I am told, in some places even in California the descendants of the mission Indians still keep up the pueblo organization as a sort of fraternity or secret society.*

In these ways, then, did the missions serve as frontier agencies of Spain. As their first and primary task the missionaries spread the Faith. But in addition, designedly or incidentally, they explored the frontiers, promoted their occupation, defended them and the interior settlements, taught the Indians the Spanish language, and disciplined them in good manners, in the rudiments of European crafts, of agriculture, and even of self-government. Moreover, the missions were a force which made for the preservation of the Indians, as opposed to their destruction, so characteristic of the Anglo-American frontier. In the English colonies the only good Indians were dead Indians. In the Spanish colonies it was thought worth while to improve the natives for this life as well as for the next. The missions did not in every respect represent a twentieth-century ideal. Sometimes, and to some degree, they failed, as is true of every human institution. Nevertheless, it must not be forgotten that of the millions of half-castes living in Latin America, the grandparents, in a large proportion of cases, at some gen-

* On January 1, 1939, I witnessed at Pisac, near Cuzco, in Peru, the installation of the new officials of the pueblo, according to the old ritual of the Spanish missions.

eration removed, on one side or the other, were once mission Indians, and as such learned the elements of Spanish civilization. For these reasons, as well as for unfeigned religious motives, the missions received the royal support. They were a conspicuous feature of Spain's frontiering genius.

THE BLACK ROBES OF
NEW SPAIN *

FOR me to appear before the American Catholic
Historical Association to speak on the subject of the
Jesuits is no less than rash. But I come with the ut-
most humility—even more than I felt when I
started to write my paper. My presence here is an
evidence of a sincere if a feeble endeavor to learn
something of the stupendous achievements of the
Black Robes in Spanish North America, and to indicate in broadest outline a field of study which a
group of us are modestly cultivating.

I

No phase of Western Hemisphere history reveals
greater heroism, and few have greater significance,
than that of the Jesuit missions. The story of the
Black Robes in Paraguay and other parts of South
America has been told by many writers. The deeds
of the Jesuits in New France have been made
widely known to English readers by the scintillat-

* A paper read at the Fifteenth Annual Meeting of the American Catholic Historical Association, December 29, 1934, Washington, D.C.

ing pages of Parkman, the monumental documentary collection edited by Thwaites, and the scholarly monographs of Kellogg and a host of Canadian scholars.

It would be presumptuous for me to attempt greatly to modify what the brilliant New England historian wrote. Indeed, aside from its limited geographical horizon and the Puritan assumptions on which it is based, the chief fault to be found with the literary masterpiece is its title. Parkman called his classic *The Jesuits in North America,* meaning only those of New France. In the book there is scarcely a hint that there were any Jesuits in colonial America except those who labored in Canada and the Mississippi Valley. He wrote so brilliantly that he conveyed to lay readers a grossly erroneous impression; for, because of Parkman's facile pen, nine out of ten persons in English speaking circles, when they hear the phrase "the Jesuits in North America," think instinctively and exclusively of the Black Robes of New France; and many of them would be surprised and perhaps skeptical if told that there were any Jesuits in colonial days other than those of whom Parkman wrote.

But the Black Robes of New France were by no means the only sons of Loyola in the North American colonies. Indeed, they were not the earliest nor the largest group, for they were long preceded and greatly outnumbered by those of New Spain. The French Jesuits suffered martyrdoms which made them justly famous among the martyrs of all the missionary world. But they were not the sole nor even the most numerous Jesuit martyrs in colonial North America, for they were far exceeded numerically by the Black Robe martyrs of Nueva España.

Judged by their own criteria, the Canadian Jesuits were not by any means the most successful sons of Loyola in colonial America. The primary aim of the missionary was to save souls. To baptize a dying babe nearly anyone of them would go through fire and water. Their first measure of success was the number of baptisms solemnized, the number of pagan mortals brought into the Christian fold. Thus computed, the success of the Canadian Jesuits was relatively small. This was no fault of theirs. They labored in a most difficult land, where Satan and his imps were particularly rampant. The Black Robes of New France counted their conversions by hundreds, or at best by thousands; those of New Spain, working in a more propitious field, numbered their baptisms by hundreds of thousands, or even by millions. And their achievements in other directions were similarly disparate.

Do not misunderstand me. These comparisons are by no means made to exalt one group of noble men in order to disparage another group equally worthy. They are intended merely to bring to the attention a momentous episode in North American history which has remained obscure. The height of one great mountain can best be realized by comparing it with another of known elevation. The imposing stature of the Jesuits of New France is widely known because they had Parkman as their historian. The Spanish Jesuits in North America await their Parkman.

There is space here only to sketch in broadest outline the two hundred year sweep of Jesuit missionary work in New Spain. What I say will be the more impressive if it is borne in mind that each page of mine calls for at least a full-length volume, each of which in turn must rest on many volumes of documentary materials, known to exist, but most of which have not been printed.[1]

II

The pioneer Jesuits in North America labored on the Atlantic seaboard, all of which was then comprised in the vast region called La Florida.[2] Father Martínez, the first Black Robe to arrive, was martyred by a Florida chief in September, 1566, just sixty years before Lallemand and his band entered Canada. Father Segura and his followers were slain near Chesapeake Bay not far from the site where the English settled thirty-six years later. Virginia history thus opened not with the founding of Jamestown, but with giving to the world eight Jesuit martyrs.

The Black Robes who escaped the Virginia massacre and a Carolina revolt were soon transferred to a happier field. Mexico, or New Spain, was made a Jesuit province. Pedro Sánchez came from Europe as Provincial with fifteen companions, who were soon joined by the Florida survivors. In the fall of 1572 Sánchez and his band reached Mexico City, and began an unbroken work of almost two centuries. Sánchez was a "sturdy beggar" and a gifted man of affairs. Generously endowed by private citizens, the viceroy, and the city, the Jesuits soon had a substantial residence and a church. More Black Robes came from Spain, an American novitiate was opened, and recruits were drawn from the "flower of Mexico."

For nearly a score of years effort was directed mainly toward establishing educational institutions, for which the young Order was already famous.[3] Four colleges and a seminary were followed by the great Colegio Máximo of San Pedro y San Pablo, which received its papal charter sixty years before Harvard opened its doors, and soon took its place as one of the three or four leading universities in all America. Father Ratkay, fresh from Europe in 1680, just before Philadelphia was founded, remarked that it had twenty-five hundred students and a respectable debt of $40,000. Schools and colleges outside Mexico City were established in quick succession, at Pátzcuaro, Valladolid, Oaxaca, Pueblo, Vera Cruz, and other places. Some of them were maintained especially for the natives. Conversion evidently bred humility, for one of the young chieftains became a professor, and taught for more than forty years in the college of San Gregorio.

Such were some of the foundations and ministries of the Black Robes in and near the capital of New Spain, among Spaniards and sedentary Indians, in the early years of their apostolate. Two decades had not passed when they began to push beyond the border to found missions among the less civilized tribes —the work in New Spain for which they ultimately became most famous.

Their maiden effort in missions *entre infieles* was at San Luís de la Paz, where they were sent to help tame the wild Chichimecos, those people who terrorized the highway leading from the capital to the mines of Zacatecas. Under the gentle influence of the Black Robes roving Indians turned to village life, warriors became farmers, and the roads were made safe. Spaniards settled in the vicinity, and the present city of San Luís de la Paz is the result. Thus the first Jesuit mission among the wild Indians of Mexico was typical of all: it became the nucleus of a Christian colony and a center of civilization.

The Chichimec mission was but a step toward the great heathendom of Nueva Vizcaya, that immense jurisdiction embracing all the country beyond Zacatecas, and extending a thousand miles or more, to New Mexico and California. Before the Jesuits arrived Spain had made considerable beginnings toward the occupation of this vast Northwest. Coronado had opened a road to Cíbola, Guzmán and Ibarra had conquered Sinaloa, thousands of cattle roamed the plains, haciendas flourished here and there in the fertile valleys, and silver mines were thinly scattered through the mountains of Durango.

Jesuit Land, for such the Northwest might well be called, comprised the modern districts of Nayarit, the four great states of Durango, Chihuahua, Sinaloa, and Sonora, Baja California, and part of Arizona, a domain larger than all of France. And the Black Robes did not merely explore this vast area, they occupied it in detail. This extensive region was chiefly a mountain country. It embraced four rather distinct geographic areas: the Central Plateau, the Sierra Madre, the Coastal Plain, and the California Peninsula, each with features which greatly influenced Jesuit activities. The Central

Plateau, seven thousand feet high in southern Durango, gradually slopes northward and extends to
and beyond the Rio Grande. On the west this table-
land is walled in by one of the roughest portions of
the entire Western Hemisphere—so rough indeed
that south of the United States border there is a
stretch of nearly a thousand miles which has never
yet been crossed by wheel track. On its precipitous
western slope this Sierra Madre is cut by numerous
rivers which tumble through immense barrancas—
veritable Grand Canyons—some of them several
thousand feet deep and many miles long. The Indians of this vast expanse were of various linguistic
stocks and of many tribes. They occupied fairly definite areas, but with a few exceptions they did not
lead a wholly sedentary life. For food most of the
mainland peoples within the area raised maize,
beans, and calabashes by primitive methods; the
Peninsula Indians practiced no agriculture at all.
The natives of the mainland coast and the foothills
were the most numerous, the most docile, and offered the best missionary field.

The pioneer missionaries in Nueva Vizcaya
were the Franciscans. But the sons of Loyola now
entered the district (1591), and became almost its
sole evangelists during the next century and three
quarters. Then the Franciscans came back. In two
wide-fronted columns the Jesuits marched north-

ward up the mainland, one up the eastern and one up the western slope of the imponderable Sierra Madre, meeting generally west of the Continental Divide. At the end of the seventeenth century they crossed the Gulf and moved in a third phalanx into the Peninsula of California.

River by river, valley by valley, canyon by canyon, tribe by tribe, these harbingers of Christian civilization advanced into the realm of heathendom. They gathered the natives into villages, indoctrinated them in the Faith, trained them in agriculture and the simpler crafts, and in schools and seminaries taught many of them reading, writing, and music. Under the tutelage of the patient Jesuits, barbarians who formerly had constructed only the meanest huts now built substantial Christian temples, some of which still stand as architectural monuments. The natives were generally well-disposed toward the missionaries. But secular Spaniards exploited their labor in mines and on haciendas; and native priests were jealous of their white competitors. The result was a series of periodic Indian revolts in which a score or more of Black Robes in New Spain won the crown of martyrdom. But the march went on.

It was a colorful pageant. Black Robes moved into the wilderness beside or ahead of prospector, miner, soldier, cattleman, and frontier trader.

[157]

Land travel was chiefly on horseback, muleback, or on foot, and land transportation by pack train or Indian carriers. As the frontier expanded, here and there a town, a mining camp, an hacienda, a garrison was pitched on the border of settlement. Still beyond, in the midst of heathendom, Christian missions were planted. As the Spaniards advanced northward, the Indians were reduced to sedentary life or were driven back. The spread of European civilization in North America was not by any means wholly a westward movement.

At the head of the Jesuit province of New Spain was the provincial, resident at Mexico City. Missions were grouped into rectorates under rectors, and these in turn into larger districts, under visitors. In regions near the capital the provincial himself customarily made the visitation. In the eighteenth century the office of visitor-general or vice-provincial was utilized. Few provincials ever found it possible to inspect the entire province.

The central feature of the mission was the pueblo, or permanent Indian village. The Black Robe went into the wilds seeking out heathen, making them his friends, telling them the Gospel story, baptizing the children of such parents as were willing, and adults who were dangerously ill. But this did not suffice. In order properly to indoctrinate the whole body of natives, drill them in the

[158]

rudiments of Christian civilization, and give them economic stability, they were assembled in pueblos, or towns, organized to achieve these aims. If the natives already lived in a permanent and compact village, there the mission was established. There the work of "reduction" had already been done. With the wilder tribes pueblo forming was often a difficult task, for they preferred to live in freedom in caves or huts. The mountain Tarahumares especially opposed reduction to pueblo life.[4] As a nucleus of a new pueblo, it was the practice to bring a few families of Christianized Indians from an older mission, to help tame and domesticate the raw recruits. Customarily each Jesuit missionary had charge of three pueblos, a *cabecera* and two *visitas*.

The heart of the mission and the pride of the padre was the church. Near by was the residence of the pastor. Close at hand, perhaps in another quadrangle, were the houses of the Indians which constituted the pueblo. In a fully developed mission there were carpenter shops, blacksmith shops, spinning and weaving rooms, corrals for the stock, fields, irrigation ditches, and everything going to make a well ordered and self supporting agricultural unit. All this was supervised by the missionary himself, assisted sometimes by a lay brother expert in the mysteries of farm and forge.

[159]

At first the buildings were of the most flimsy character. These in time were replaced by more substantial houses, larger and more beautiful churches, generally of adobe but sometimes of stone. In hostile country it was customary to erect a strong protecting wall around the pueblo, or at least around the missionary's residence, and to provide it with military towers. Such a mission was a veritable frontier stronghold. To help supervise the labor of the Indians, keep them in order, punish minor offenses, and drill the neophytes in the rudiments of civilized life, native officers were appointed—governor, captain, alcalde, topil, mador, chief herdsman, head muleteer, head plowman, etc. According to their respective spheres, some of these functionaries were named by the missionary, others by the provincial governor or some other secular representative of the king.[5]

Religious teaching of the neophytes included a daily routine of drill in the catechism, prayers, and sacred music. Many a missionary was as proud of his native choir and orchestra as of his church.[6] Promising youths were trained as altar boys, and as *temastianes* or catechists, to help drill the neophytes. Several of the central missions—those at San Felipe, Mátape, Parral, Chihuahua, and other places—had seminaries designed to give the temastianes the necessary training for their tasks. The religious life of a mission included attendance at Mass, the regular prayers, the Sunday sermon, confession, and the celebration of Church holidays with processions, pageantry, and other suitable exercises, in imitation of the Spanish settlements. These religious fiestas, often attended by the Spaniards of the vicinity, were combined with the jollities of secular sports—foot races, horse races, bull fights, and other healthful releases for the nervous system. On his own testimony one Black Robe, at least, is known to have engaged in a race with his Indians—he on horseback, they on foot—and to have been beaten.

III

The pioneer Jesuit in Nueva Vizcaya was Gonzalo de Tapia, of eternal fame.[7] With one companion in 1591 he crossed the perilous Sierra Madre. His precise destination was San Felipe, on Sinaloa River, then the very last outpost of European civilization in northwestern New Spain. San Felipe became and long continued to be the Jesuit capital on the Pacific Coast. Taking their lives in their hands, the two apostles undertook their gigantic task. Their touch was magic. Within six months several pueblos had been formed and more than a thousand natives baptized. Undaunted by poisoned arrows and yawning chasms, Tapia re-crossed the Sierra to Mexico for additional help. More workers came, other thousands were converted, new pueblos established and better churches built.

Four years passed, and the Faith was taking firm root on Sinaloa River. But in the same degree, the chronicler tells us, the wrath of Satan grew. Tapia was marked for destruction. Nacabeba, a native medicine man, who saw his power waning, brained Father Gonzalo with a war club and celebrated his triumph with pagan orgies. Tapia thus became the proto-martyr of Jesuit New Spain. It was a terrible shock to the Black Robes, but the work went on. The confidence of the natives regained, conversions struck a new pace. By the end of the first decade there had been 10,000 baptisms, and the Jesuits had eight missions with substantial churches serving thirteen pueblos along Sinaloa and Mocorito Rivers.

People sometimes raise their eyebrows at such stories of wholesale baptisms at the beginning. But the explanation is simple. Infant heathen were baptized without catechism, the same as children of Christians. When the padres first arrived there was a large crop of infants awaiting them. Thereafter baptisms proceeded at a slower rate, for the annual increment of babes was smaller than the first accumulation; and older children and adults must first be instructed.

Almost simultaneously the Black Robes began their work on both slopes and in the heart of the Sierra Madre. With a gift of $22,000 from Governor del Rio and others, a college was established in Durango in 1593–4. By the end of the century six Jesuits of this house were founding missions among the Acaxees in Topia, among the Tepehuanes in central Durango, and at Parras among the Laguna tribes of Coahuila. Here was a field as large as that of Sinaloa.

Father Santarén became the saint of Topia; but Ruíz did not fall far behind him in prowess and fame. Together they assembled crowds, destroyed heathen idols, built churches, and baptized thousands. At first the natives were friendly. But Topia was a mining district, Indian labor was exploited, and a typical revolt followed. The Acaxees took up arms, murdered Spaniards, burned churches, and devastated mining towns. In the crisis Father Ruíz performed a prodigy. Eight hundred Acaxees besieged forty Spaniards at San Andrés. The beleaguered settlers struck back. In one of the sorties Ruíz marched ahead of the soldiers protected only by his crucifix. "Clouds of arrows were discharged at the holy man, but not one struck him," we are told. The chronicler regarded this as evidence of divine protection—a scoffer might suspect bad native marksmanship.

Governor Urdiñola rushed from Durango with soldiers to relieve the siege. But Santarén became the hero of the episode. Going almost alone among the hostiles, by diplomacy he won them over and marched back to Topia at the head of a thousand natives bearing a cross and the white flag of peace. There was a love feast and the Indians rebuilt their churches. The conversion now spread to the Ximes and other tribes, where there were baptisms by added thousands. The name of Santarén is still a household word in all that western Sierra, where he has become a legendary figure.

Fonte and Ramírez had parallel success in central and northern Durango among the virile Tepehuanes. Other evangelists turned northeast and founded missions in the famous lake region of Coahuila called Parras. The Lake People were docile and the progress of the Black Robes was flattering. But like other missions, those of Parras had their full measure of pioneer troubles. Smallpox carried off four hundred neophytes in 1608, shortly before Jamestown's "starving time." The Nazas River went on a rampage, destroyed the church of one mission, forced the people to flee from another, and nearly cost the life of a Black Robe. First it was too wet, then too dry. Drought

[164]

was followed by famine. But in spite of these calamities baptisms multiplied to thousands, and Parras became a precious jewel in Loyola's crown.

The scene now shifts back to Sinaloa.[8] On nearly every frontier the Black Robes found and relied on some secular champion. Such were Del Rio and Urdiñola in Durango. More famous in this rôle was Hurdaide, defender of the Faith in Sinaloa, contemporary of Canada's Champlain, of Virginia's John Smith, and of Plymouth's John Alden. His appointment as Captain at San Felipe was a decisive event in Sinaloa history and in Jesuit annals. For nearly three decades this bandy-legged soldier ruled the Pacific Coast like a mediæval Count of the March. El Capitán, as he was known, was famous far and wide for the wax seals with which he authenticated his orders. Any naked Indian messenger bearing a bit of paper stamped with these symbols had safe passage among friends or foes.

Hurdaide's part was to make safe the northward advance of the Black Robes. The Sinaloa River vineyard had been firmly planted by Tapia and his successors. But the way to the Fuerte, the next main stream north, was blocked by hostile Suaquis, Sinaloas, and Tehuecos. One by one El Capitán subdued these tribes, by methods which were sometimes harsh and always spectacular. Fathers Ribas,

Méndez, and Villalta followed where Hurdaide led. Ribas made his name enduring at Ahome, Villalta baptized four hundred Sinaloas the very first day, Méndez gleaned a similar harvest, and within a year the whole river valley west of the mountains had been added to Christendom. By placating the sturdy Yaquis and subduing the defiant mountain Tepahues, El Capitán next opened the way to Mayo River. Venerable Father Méndez, once more in the vanguard, headed a procession of Black Robes, three thousand children were baptized within two weeks, and seven pueblos were founded in a stretch of eighteen leagues. The 30,000 Mayos had come into the fold.

All the North Country now received a terrific shock, and mountain streams of Durango ran red with the blood of missionaries and settlers. In the Tepehuán missions the Black Robes had labored with gratifying success for more than two decades. Pueblos had been formed, churches built, thousands of Indians baptized. Then suddenly the Tepehuanes, led by a self-styled Messiah, rose in savage rebellion. In the fall of 1616 the natives of Santa Catalina sprung the trap and murdered Father Tobar. Two hundred Spaniards fell at Atotonilco, one of the victims being the Franciscan Father Gutiérrez. At Santiago Papasquiaro Fathers Orozco and Cisneros, with some Spanish

[166]

families, were brutally slain in the cemetery. At Zape nearly a hundred victims fell, including Fathers Alavez, Del Valle, Fonte, and Moranta. Santarén, the saint of Topia, who happened to be in the vicinity, also went down in this bloody uprising. Soldiers hurried north, punished rebels, gathered up the remains of the martyred missionaries, and took them to Durango, where they were buried with solemn honors. The Tepehuán rebellion was at an end. Undaunted, new Black Robes entered the field, and the missions were restored.

On the West Coast the missions now entered upon the period of their greatest prosperity. The Tepehuán revolt had caused uneasiness in Sinaloa, lest the still heathen Yaquis should join the rebels. Instead they welcomed the Black Robes in their own territory and became one of the most faithful Christian communities. Ribas moved up the map once more and became the apostle to this dauntless tribe, among whom he set up the Cross in May, 1617. Four thousand children and five hundred adults were baptized within a few weeks. More workers came, eight missions were founded, and soon most of the populous tribe were converted. As a granary for sterile California, these Yaqui missions later played a distinctive rôle.

From the Yaquis it was but a step to the Lower Pimas and Opatas, higher up on the Yaqui River, where flourishing missions were begun in 1620, year of the Mayflower. Venerable Méndez, like Daniel Boone, ever on the frontier, went into the mountains to the Sahuaripas. Azpilcueto, at Batuco, was a fighting padre long remembered in this region. Hostile neighbors threatened to kill him and drive away his fellow Jesuits. "Hurry up" was the message he sent them; then he coolly awaited their approach. When he fired a musket and brandished a machete they turned and fled, to return soon afterward as loyal neophytes. By now the Sinaloa-Sonora missions had reached impressive proportions. Baptisms there in 1621 alone were over 17,000. As a consequence of the great expansion a new rectorate was formed in the north with its capital at the Yaqui town of Tórin, where the thick-walled old Jesuit church on the hill, today in ruins, looks like a Roman fortress. The rectorate at this time employed eleven Black Robes, and embraced 60,000 Mayos, Yaquis, and Lower Pimas. On the whole West Coast there were 86,340 converts in fifty-five pueblos. Three years later the number was estimated at more than 100,000.

Several veterans now left the scene. In 1620 Ribas retired after sixteen years on the coast, to become provincial in Mexico and to write his great history. Six years later died Martín Pérez, veteran

[168]

of all the West, for he had come with Tapia, the Founder. At the same time Sinaloa lost by death its matchless soldier, El Capitán Hurdaide. Few regions in America have had more colorful pioneers than these. Notwithstanding the loss of the Old Guard—or perhaps because of it, for Old Guards have a way of becoming impedimenta— the boom in the West continued. At Chínipas, high up in the barranca-gouged mountains, Julio Pascual won several thousand converts. In 1623 he was joined by Father Martínez. As he climbed the mountain trail to his new destination, Martínez unwittingly rode to his death. A week after his arrival both he and Pascual were martyred by hostile Chief Cambeia. The Chínipas mission was now closed, to be reopened four decades later.

Martyrdom but fanned the apostolic flame. The Black Robes now pushed on to Valle de Sonora, and to the upper waters of the many-forked Yaqui, thus carrying the Gospel to the border of the lands of the Apaches and the Upper Pimas. Valle de Sonora, site of Coronado's ill-fated San Gerónimo, was the most historic spot in all that mountain-girt region. It is from this charming little valley, peopled by gentle and industrious Opatas, that the vast state of Sonora gets its name. Father Castaño came here to live among the Opatas in 1638, shortly after Roger Williams fled to his Rhode

Island wilderness. Within a year Castaño had baptized three thousand natives, who lived in pueblos which still bear the names by which they then were known. More Jesuits came. Soon the northernmost missions, mainly of Opatas, were formed into a new rectorate,[9] where seven Jesuits were ministering to fourteen pueblos, and in which already there had been a total of more than 20,000 baptisms. *Fervet opus,* the chronicler wrote.

Paraguay itself could scarcely match this evangelical record. When Ribas published his famous *Triumphos de Nuestra Santa Fee* in 1645, the showing for a half century of labor was most impressive. West of the Sierra, in the stretch of some six hundred miles, there were now thirty-five head missions, each with from one to four towns, perhaps a hundred in all. Each of the head missions and many of the *visitas,* or substations, had fine churches, prosperous farms and well-stocked ranches. The mission books showed a total of more than 300,000 baptisms in the West to date. The presidio of San Felipe, the principal garrison, had a force of only forty-six soldiers. This fact alone, Bancroft remarks, shows how completely the natives had accepted missionary control.

Again the scene shifts. The Jesuit frontier west of the Sierra Madre had far outrun that on the eastern slope, a fact which may be explained in part by three circumstances. The Tepehuán revolt had caused a setback on the Central Plateau; hostile Tobosos and Conchos made mission life precarious there; and the field was partly covered by the Franciscans, who were active on the right flank of the Jesuits. But the Black Robes now made a new thrust forward, to work among the Tarahumares, those fleet-footed mountain people who lived on both slopes of the Sierra Madre in western Chihuahua. Before his martyrdom Fonte had made a small beginning there, and another nibble at the same bait was taken in 1630. Nine years later the Tarahumar missions were begun in earnest. Meanwhile the prosperous mining town of Parral was founded (1632) and became for a century the residence of the governors of Nueva Vizcaya. For that reason it played a vital part in subsequent Jesuit history.

Gerónimo Figueroa and José Pascual launched the New Deal for the Tarahumares in 1639 (year of the Fundamental Orders of Connecticut), when they founded missions on Conchos River north and west of Parral. A corps of Black Robes followed in their train, reaped a large harvest, and by 1650 carried the Cross north and west to the upper Yaqui River in Tarahumara Alta. But they had come to a most difficult frontier, quite different from that of Sonora. The incursions of wild

Tobosos made life unsafe for priest, soldier, or neophyte. Then the Tarahumares themselves, led by haughty Chief Tepóraca, rose in revolt, destroyed several missions, murdered Father Godínez (Beudin) at Papigóchic, and massacred all the Spanish settlers at the nearby town of Aguilar. The city of Guerrero marks the approximate site today. In a second onslaught Father Basile was decapitated and hanged to a cross. Legend has it that as he expired his spirit, in the form of a beautiful child, was seen to issue from his mouth and ascend to Heaven attended by two angels. Thus was lengthened the list of Jesuit martyrs. With a courage which commands more than admiration, the Black Robes soon reoccupied the southern missions. But with Papigóchic destroyed, Tarahumara Alta, the region of the high Sierra, was still solidly heathen.

For two decades the Tarahumar field remained stationary. Then another forward movement was begun in 1673. This, by the way, was the very year when Marquette reached the Mississippi River. French and Spanish Black Robes were approaching each other from opposite sides of the continent. The Tarahumara Alta missions were now reopened. Apostles Tardá and Guadalajara entered the Sierra as far as Yepómera and Tutuaca. The region was inconceivably difficult; mountains and

barrancas were inexpressibly rough; only the
hardiest men could endure the winter cold. Yet the
missions flourished. Eight Jesuits in Tarahumara
Alta were serving 4,000 natives in thirty-two pueblos in 1678, and within the next four years more
than thirty new churches were built.

New names now appear on the honor roll. Foronda and Picolo, Neumann and Ratkay, led a procession of Black Robes from Italy and North Europe who greatly vitalized the work. For ten years
they toiled on in the midst of privation and danger. Then another revolt burst forth. There was a
gold rush to Santa Rosa, and Spaniards summoned
the Indians to forced labor. It was the story of
Papigóchic repeated. In 1690 the natives murdered Fathers Foronda and Sánchez, expelled
the rest of the Black Robes from the Sierra, and
destroyed six mountain missions.[10] But peace was
restored, the fearless Jesuits returned to their
mountain exile, and rebuilt their churches "larger
and better than before." Seven years later peace
was disturbed by an outburst of native wizardry.
This was precisely the time when witchcraft was
epidemic in New England. If we can believe the
evidence, broom voyages then were more numerous than airplane flights today. Feminism seems
to have been at the zero hour in Tarahumara, for
nothing is said of witches. But many wizards were

[173]

captured and executed, for Spaniards were as silly as Englishmen or Germans of their day. The result was another uprising. Rebels destroyed four mountain missions and again the Jesuits fled. War was followed by the submission of the natives, and the return of the Black Robes to their posts.

It had been a bitter conflict. However, says Father Neumann, who was in the midst of it all, not half of the Tarahumar nation had taken up arms or deserted Christianity.[11] The whole situation was now changed by a new Indian policy. Henceforth little effort was made to move Tarahumares from their mountain homes to the plains. Henceforth they remained peaceful, and the Jesuits went forward with their apostolic labors among them. The circumstance carries a moral—the transplantation policy had been a mistake from the outset.

On the eastern edge of the Tarahumara, Chihuahua became a flourishing city and the seat of a Jesuit college, where a lay brother wrote a widely used treatise on medicine. Among the colorful Black Robes in the Tarahumara at a later date was Glandorff, who served some forty years at Tomochic. Famous for his gentle sanctity, he was even better known as the great hiker. He was afraid of a horse, but he could climb a mountain like a goat, and in a cross-country run would put a mule to blush. He was a marvel even to the fleet-footed Tarahumares, who even today have world-wide renown for their own speed and endurance. According to legend Glandorff had magic shoes. An Indian servant worn with travel fell exhausted. Glandorff loaned him his moccasins and behold, he sprang up revived as if from a refreshing sleep, and without further halt continued his journey! This happened not once but many times. So runs the diverting legend.

Other frontiers were pushing forward. The Chínipas missions, after a blank of four decades, were restored by the Italians Prado and Pecora in 1676, just when Tardá and Guadalajara were re-viving the work in Tarahumara Alta. At the end of four years they had gathered into pueblos and converted 4,000 Indians. Square-jawed Salva-tierra now joined his countrymen in the district, and became its most distinguished missionary. One of his exploits was his descent into the mammoth can-yon of Urique, in size and awesomeness a close competitor of the Grand Canyon of the Colorado. His naïve account of the adventure is refreshing. With a Cerocahui Indian he set forth to visit the stupendous gorge. The guide told him he could ride three leagues, then he would have to walk. This admonition proved unnecessary. "On seeing the precipice," says Salvatierra, "such was my terror that I immediately asked . . . if it was time to dismount. Without waiting for an answer I did not dismount but let myself fall off on the side opposite the precipice, sweating and trembling all over from fright. For there opened on the left a chasm whose bottom could not be seen, and on the right rose perpendicular walls of solid rock." He was on a mantel shelf suspended in mid-air. This account by Father Juan in 1684 should help deflate the egotism of twentieth-century "discoverers" of Urique canyon.

For ten years Salvatierra labored in the mountains, then went humbly to Guadalajara as college president. Seven years later, when on the way to Lower California, he made a flying trip to his beloved Guazápares, just in time to help check another rebellion. Not Salvatierra alone, but Fathers Ordaz and Illing likewise won fame in this war, one as a valiant defender of his mission, the other as an equally brave peacemaker. Each one left a precious legend in the land of the Chínipas.

The northwestward tide was now deflected. By this time the Black Robes had established Christianity in the Sierra Madre and on both its slopes, all the way from southern Durango to northern Chihuahua, and from Culiacán to the Arizona border. On the northeast they were blocked by the Apaches as by a Chinese wall. But the way was open to the west and northwest, in Lower California and in Pimería Alta, where large and friendly populations lay still beyond the rim of Christendom. To cultivate these extensive vineyards now came Kino, Campos, Salvatierra, Ugarte, and a valiant host of only less notable figures. Conspicuous among them all was Kino, Apostle to Pimería Alta. He arrived there in March, 1687, the very month when La Salle met his tragic death in the wilds of Texas. He was just well started when the Pimas destroyed several missions and martyred Father Saeta at Caborca. But for a quarter-century he kept on. He personally baptized more than 4,500 Indians.[12] His mission farms and ranches became the most prosperous in all Sonora. His demonstration that Lower California was a peninsula, not an island, reversed stubborn opinion. Of Pimería Alta he was not only Apostle, but also explorer, ethnologist, cartographer, defender, cattle king, and historian.

With his dream of converting Lower California, Father Kino infected Salvatierra, who translated the vision into reality. The peninsula was assigned to the Jesuits on condition that they finance it themselves. In return they were made practically autonomous, like their brethren in Paraguay. Aided by the giant athlete Ugarte, Salvatierra raised and organized the celebrated Pious Fund,

[177]

which is still in existence. Thus financed, he maintained a little fleet of transports which plied back and forth across the Gulf, carrying livestock and other supplies for barren Lower California, obtained chiefly from the mainland Black Robes. By the time of his death he and his associates had founded seven flourishing missions among almost savage Indians, on a rocky tongue of land scarcely capable of sustaining civilized life.

Ugarte now carried the Cross to the hostile people on the lower end of the Peninsula, where the names of Carranco and Tamaral were added to the already long list of Jesuit martyrs. In the mid-century new foundations were made in the north, until nearly a score of successful missions were in operation, and many thousand Indians were settled in pueblo life. During their stay of seventy years in Lower California, more than fifty Black Robes, all told, labored in exile on this barren cactus patch.

The last three Lower California missions were made possible by a Borgian heiress. The tale is told that when she made the gift she was asked in what country she wished the missions established. "In the most outlandish place in the world," she replied. The Jesuits consulted their atlases and returned the answer: "The most outlandish place in all the world is California." So there the new missions were planted.

The early eighteenth century witnessed a great shortage of missionaries. European wars drained the Spanish treasury. Then came a remarkable revival. In the far south the Black Robes took over the difficult Coras of Nayarit. In the north a new missionary host, mainly Germans, entered the field on both sides of the Gulf. In Sonora and Pimería Alta the Jesuit annals record the eighteenth-century labors of Black Robes with the very un-Spanish names of Bentz, Fraedenberg, Gerstner, Grashofer, Hoffenrichter, Hawe, Keller, Klever, Kolub, Kürtzel, Middendorff, Miner, Nentwig, Och, Paver, Rhuen, Sedelmayr, Segesser, Slesac, Step, Steiger, Wazet, and Weis. In Lower California in these days labored Baegert, Bischoff, Consag, Ducrue, Gasteiger, Gordon, Helen, Link, Neumayer, Retz, Tempis, Tuersch, and Wagner, all of non-Spanish extraction. In the transplanting of Christian culture to Western America these North Europeans played a distinctive part. Zealous missionaries, they were especially conspicuous as teachers of material thrift and a well ordered life.

By these men Kino's old missions were restored and new ones founded. Keller and Sedelmayr re-

[179]

traced some of Kino's trails to the Gila and the Colorado Rivers. They, Consag, and Link revived Kino's plan to extend missions to the Colorado, and to supply Lower California by a land route around the head of the Gulf. In the midst of their labors the Pimas rose once more in rebellion, and killed Tello at Caborca and Rhuen at Sonóita. The West Coast martyrs now numbered one more than a score.

A large missionary province, the result of many years of development, was like a tree. The fresh growth was near the top. So it was with the Province of New Spain. The roots of the plant were the central organization in Europe and Mexico. The colleges and other permanent foundations at the principal centers on the way north represented the trunk. As time went on, this trunk gradually became bare of missionary verdure. Between Durango and Pimería Alta in the eighteenth century there were missions in all stages of evolution, some already secularized, others old and stable, but without new blood from heathendom; still others, on the periphery, filled with the vigor characteristic of youth.

The Jesuits had always labored under a degree of insecurity due to causes other than Indian revolts. Frequently there was pressure for secularizing the missions, a step which was contemplated

[180]

in the system. This pressure came from bishops for various reasons, from the government which wished to collect tribute, or from secular neighbors who were greedy for Indian lands or the right to exploit Indian labor. In the middle eighteenth century the missions among the Tepehuanes and in Tarahumara Baja were thus turned over to the parish clergy.

Then came the final blow—the Expulsion. For reasons best known to himself and his advisers, Carlos III decided to expel the Jesuits from the whole of the Spanish empire. The edict fell in 1767. All missionaries and other Black Robes in New Spain were arrested, dispossessed, hurried to Vera Cruz, carried to Spain, imprisoned there, or distributed in other lands. Many of the expatriates died of disease or hardship on the way. Some of the missions thus left vacant were secularized, others were put in charge of the Franciscans. Here is where Serra comes into the California story. A work of two centuries was at an end. But the service of the Black Robes to the land of their toil did not cease even now. Many of them spent their prison hours writing of the country they loved. Clavigero composed his history of California, Baegert his *Nachrichten,* Pfefferkorn his book on Sonora, Ducrue his story of the expulsion from the Peninsula. These and other works were published. Still others remain in manuscript and await the modern historian, for whom they will constitute a fresh fountain of inspiration and knowledge.

IV

Thus far this paper has been devoted to sketching in broadest outline the work of the Jesuits in New Spain, with special reference to the northward advance of the missionary frontier. The deep significance of it all would call for another paper of equal or greater length. There is space here for only a few observations.

The Black Robe story is one of Homeric quality. It is filled with picturesque men, like Santarén, who vied with the Pied Piper of Hamelin; Ruíz, who was arrow proof; Azpilcueto, who bluffed an Indian horde with blunderbuss and machete; Contreras, who led the defense of Cocóspera against an Apache attack; Kino, the hard-riding cowman; Glandorff, the Black Robe hiker with the magic shoes. The tale is full of diverting humor and of exalting edification. The actors were human beings, who either had a sense of humor or were humorous because they lacked it.

These missionaries were the adventurers of the seventeenth and eighteenth centuries, successors to the conquistadores of an earlier day. They traveled vast distances, coped with rugged nature and the fickle savage, performed astounding physical feats, won amazing victories over mountains, rivers, hunger, cold, and thirst.

Missionary life demanded the highest qualities of manhood—character, intelligence, courage, resourcefulness, health, and endurance. Missionaries were called upon to face physical dangers and hardships almost beyond belief. They went among heathen without escorts, into places where soldiers dared not tread. They were liable at any time to hear the blood-curdling war whoop or to see the destroying fire by night. They were ever at the mercy of the whims of sensitive Indians, or of jealous and vengeful medicine men. Even to baptize a child was often perilous, for if it died the death might be charged to the "bad medicine" of the padre. Martyrdom was always a very distinct possibility. Most Black Robes came to America hoping to win this glorious crown, many still coveted it after seeing real Indians, and when martyrdom stared them in the face they met it with transcendent heroism.

Their hardest trial, more to be feared than death, was loneliness, for they lived many leagues apart and saw their own kind only at long intervals. Hence they treasured visits from distant neighbors, and looked forward with the eagerness of a homesick boy to the church dedications and celebrations which brought them for a brief time together; or to the annual journey to a neighbor mission to fulfill their religious obligations.

Not every Black Robe was fit for service in the missions. Some lacked the temperament or the physical stamina, some could not learn the Indian languages. Such were given employment of a different sort. More than one Jesuit who found himself unsuited for the frontier was sent to be professor or president in some college in softer surroundings. Many of these Jesuits had in their veins the best blood of Europe. Such were Hernando Tobar, grand-nephew of Viceroy Mendoza; Pedro Velasco, relative of another viceroy; Ratkay, the Hungarian noble who had been a page at the Court of Vienna; and Salvatierra, son of a noble house of Spain and Italy. The Black Robes belonged to their age. They had an unfaltering faith in God and His omnipotence. Miracles were not only possible, but often passed before their eyes. They believed in and talked much of predestination. Indeed, they recognized it every time they came upon and baptized a dying ancient. The man and his wife, each two hundred and fifty years old, who were baptized by Ribas, were clear examples of this exercise of divine mercy, by which two lives were extended till the evangelist arrived.

Being theologians and spiritual practitioners, the Black Robes were naturally interested in all religious and spiritual phenomena. True to their day, they believed not only in a personal God, but also in a personal Devil, the same Devil so well known to Cotton Mather. The missionaries saw all around them patent evidence of the malice and of the mischief done by His Satanic Majesty and his obedient imps. They believed in signs and portents. Eclipses, earthquakes, epidemics, and all unusual phenomena were interpreted as divine or diabolic manifestations, with supernatural cause and significance. Witchcraft was taken for granted by seventeenth-century Jesuits, and its evils were often encountered, just as was the case in Puritan New England and in all contemporary Europe. Spaniards brought with them all the European phraseology of witchcraft, and the usual machinery for rooting it out.

A catalogue of the manifold services of the missionaries would be long and varied. In their daily routine, like the monks of old, they performed the most menial tasks. They cooked, washed, plowed, planted, harvested, handled stock, made adobes, built houses and erected churches. They served as

[185]

nurses and doctors in the huts of natives. During epidemics they were called from pillar to post, lacking time even to eat or sleep. "For in these missions," says Father Neumann, "there is but one craftsman: the missionary himself. He alone must serve both himself and others. He must be cobbler, tailor, mason, carpenter, cook, nurse for the sick —in a word, everything."

The Black Robes converted the natives to Christianity, baptizing in New Spain alone, before the expulsion, probably not less than two millions. They also brought to the Indians the rudiments of Christian civilization, teaching them decent habits, agriculture, stock raising, the handicrafts, building, and myriad other things. The less civilized natives were the ones most remolded by mission life.

A comparison will again help us. The Jesuits of New France played a highly important part in the religious, educational, and social life of the French part of the colony. But by reason of circumstances beyond their control, they did relatively little toward transforming the society of the Indian population of the vast areas over which they traveled. The Jesuits of New Spain, on the other hand, were primary agents during a century and three-quarters in the transformation of a large native population from a roving to a sedentary life, with attendant cultural changes. Indeed, a considerable part of the inhabitants of western Mexico today are descended from ancestors, on one side or the other, who got their first contact with European civilization as neophytes in a Jesuit mission. That this was possible in one case and not in the other, was due largely to the contrasting views of the respective nations under whom the Jesuits worked. Spain considered the Indian worth civilizing as well as converting, and proceeded with zeal and firmness to bring it about. In the process the missionaries were the government's best collaborators.

The Black Robes performed many services for the border Spaniards as well as for the neophytes. The mission was the agricultural unit for a large part of frontier Spanish America. There the missionary organized and directed most of the agricultural labor. The mission not only raised produce for its own subsistence, but from the surplus it supplied neighboring soldiers, miners and cattlemen with agricultural products. The missionaries, by gentle means, subdued and managed the Indians, went as diplomats to hostile tribes, and helped to pacify the frontier in time of trouble. The mission itself, with its fortified plant and its usually loyal native defenders, often served as a bulwark against hostile neighbors. Regarding frontier matters, religious or secular, including in-

[187]

ternational relations, the missionaries helped to mold the opinions of central officials, and were often called to Mexico, or even to Spain and Rome, to give advice. Instructions issued from Europe on such matters were both shaped and interpreted by the men on the frontier, for they were the ones who best knew conditions.

The importance of the Black Robes as teachers and founders of colleges has been touched upon in earlier paragraphs. Their scholarly services were not confined to teaching. They wrote learned books on a great variety of subjects. Incidentally to their frontier work they were explorers, cartographers and ethnologists. Ribas declared them linguists by divine gift, and certain it is that they did much to reduce to grammar and to preserve the languages of many tribes, some of which have long since disappeared.

Finally, the Jesuits were the principal historians of early western North America. Pérez de Ribas, Kino, Venegas, Alegre, Ortega, Baegert, Pfefferkorn and the author of the *Rudo Ensayo* all wrote chronicles which will never be displaced. The Black Robes of New France left us as a legacy the famous Jesuit *Relations* which were assembled by Cramoisy and put into English by Thwaites. These ample records of life in the wilderness are justly celebrated among the treasures of pioneer days in heathen America. They constitute a precious body of historical literature. Equally precious in quality and vastly greater in bulk are the similar Jesuit writings left behind by the Black Robes of New Spain. Most of these have yet to be assembled and edited, a gigantic task toward which a few students are now directing their attention.

[1] In preparing a sketch so broad and so general as this one, it has not been deemed advisable to give specific citations to all the materials drawn upon. Besides the general authorities such as Florencia, Pérez de Ribas, Alegre, Manje, Kino, Venegas, Baegert, Pfefferkorn, Decorme, Astrain, and Bancroft, extensive use has been made of documentary materials from foreign archives, most of which are still unpublished. It is a pleasure to acknowledge here the stimulus which I have received in my study of Jesuit history from my former students, the Reverend Dr. William Eugene Shiels, S.J., the Reverend Dr. Jerome V. Jacobsen, S.J., and the Reverend Dr. Peter M. Dunne, S.J.

[2] Their story has just been told in an excellent volume by the Reverend Dr. Michael Kenny, S.J., entitled *The Romance of the Floridas.*

[3] The Reverend Dr. Jerome V. Jacobsen, S.J., will soon make known this important chapter in the history of America in a book, now awaiting publication, entitled *Educational Foundations of the Jesuits in New Spain.* [Published in 1938 by the University of California Press, Berkeley].

[4] The difficulties of gathering these mountain people into pueblos are set forth by Father Joseph Neumann in a letter written during his first months among them: "Our labors consist in converting and baptizing the natives, in founding settlements, in persuading the Indians to leave their caves and scattered hovels and to adopt a civilized life, and in forming them, so to speak,

[189]

into a corporate body. We compel them to live in villages near the churches, which we build in convenient locations where the country is more open. This is a very difficult task. For,—to explain their character a little—while these people were still heathen . . . they were accustomed to live, not in groups, but separated, one from another. With their wives and children they dwelt in mountain caves or in huts built of straw, which seemed more suitable for catching birds than for human habitation." (Letter to an unknown Father, Sisoguichic, Feb. 8, 1682.)

[5] Father Pfefferkorn, long a missionary in Sonora, thus describes the functions of the *madores* in a book which he wrote after the Jesuit Expulsion: "In each pueblo there were also one or two *mayori* or, as the Spaniards say, *madores,* who had the supervision of the grown children and at the same time the care of the sick. For this office Indians were chosen who from their known behavior gave promise of being faithful and careful. . . . They assembled the children daily for attendance at Mass and the Christian service, and during it they watched that order and decency be maintained. They also visited daily all the houses in the pueblo to see if there was anybody ill within. If they saw that anybody was in the least danger they immediately informed the pastor, who then had a look for himself and acted according to the circumstances. Marriages, which for most important reasons were arranged as soon as the age of the Indians permitted, were usually managed by the *mayor.* He chose the pair whom he thought suited to one another and presented them to the pastor. The latter inquired into the views of both parties and if they agreed the marriage took place." Pfefferkorn describes also the functions of pueblo governors, alcaldes, and fiscales. (*Beschreibung des Landschaft Sonora,* Cologne, 1795.) This important work is being edited for publication in English by Dr. Theodore Treutlein.

[6] Pfefferkorn writes as follows: "In all the missions of the Opatas and Eudebes, also in some among the Pimas, Solemn High Mass was celebrated on Sundays and feast days. Some of

the choirs consisted of Indians who were so skillful in singing that many European churches might well wish such choristers. I had eight of them in my mission of Cucurpe, four men and four women. Among the latter one especially was noted for her incomparable voice. In the missions of the Opatas and Eudebes there were also Indians who performed with very agreeable harmony on musical instruments and who during Mass played in the pauses when the singers stopped. Mine practiced so diligently under my direction that they accompanied the singers with violins, harps, and zithers. In this way in my mission we not only celebrated Mass, but in the evening, after the completion of the Christian Doctrine and the saying of the Rosary, we sang the Litany of Loretto and the *Salve Regina,* accompanied by instruments."

[7] His inspiring career has recently been made known to English readers through the excellent biography by Father William Eugene Shiels, entitled *Gonzalo de Tapia* (1561–1594).

[8] In a forthcoming book on the Jesuit missions of Sinaloa Rev. Dr. Peter M. Dunne has taken up the story where Father Shiels left off.

[9] This was in 1646.

[10] Yepómera, Tutuaca, Cahurichic, Tomochic, Mátachic, and Cocomorachic.

[11] Neumann, Joseph, *Historia Seditionum,* etc., Prague. No date on the title page. The preface is dated April 15, 1724. This work is being edited for publication in English by Dr. Allen Christelow, of Oxford University.

[12] Not 40,000, as every writer insists on saying, because they follow Ortega, who misread Kino's manuscript.

(1)